YOUNG WRITERS

ALL ABOARD FOR

ESSEX

First published in Great Britain in 1995 by
POETRY NOW
1-2 Wainman Road, Woodston,
Peterborough, PE2 7BU

All Rights Reserved

Copyright Contributors 1995

SB ISBN 1 85731 735 1

Foreword

Toot, Toot! All Aboard! Set sail on a fantastic journey through the minds of today's children. Along the way we hope you will be charmed and enlightened by the thoughts, feelings and humour expressed by these young writers.

The poems included in this anthology have been selected for their exciting imagination, depth of feelings and down to earth language; revealing these children's awareness of various important issues close to many of our hearts. Now you can finally find out what these children *really* think of their parents, teachers and why trees lose their leaves in autumn!

We hope that you will sit back and enjoy this on-board entertainment, and we wish you a pleasant journey. Bon voyage!

CONTENTS

Arthur Bugler Junior School

Manjinder Dhillon	1
Jenny Addis	1
Jade Ahmed	2
Leanne Petitt	2
Victoria Bienvenu	3
Jemma Gale	3
Laura Hutchinson	4
Carly Merritt	4
Gemma Louise McGill	4
Georgia Weekes	5
Hayley Rawson	5
James Hunter	6
Wendy Hickford	6
Samantha Mallia	7
Richard Hollington	7
Joseph Galer	8

Bancroft's School, Preparatory Department

Christopher Straker	8
Nikki Walsh	9
Jason Gerlis	9
Jessica Charlesworth	10
Eleanor Lear	10
Sandipan Bhowmik	11
Saul Dindol	11
Shama Naqushbandi	12
Victoria Wojewodka	12
Anna Maddox	13

Beckers Green School

Ruth Boatwright	14
Sean Mark Attwood	14
Larnce Forrester	15
Elener Ambrose	15
Serena Dunne	16
Charlotte Twaites	16
Nikki Clark	17
Tony Robert Hardy	17

	Kate Coxell	17
	Leah Ashdown	18
	Charlotte West	18
Beehive Lane CP School		
	Emma Catterall	19
	Roy Clancy	19
	Louise Swinney	19
	Adam Brewster	20
	Jennifer Mack	20
Blenheim CP School		
	Matthew Fowler	21
Boxted C of E Primary School		
	Richard Woolener	21
	James Brooks	22
	Dora Steel	22
Boys' High School, Colchester		
	Paul Wiggins	23
	James Maxfield	23
	Mark Stobbs	24
	Ben Russell	24
	Tim France	25
	Tobias Larsen	25
Brightside Junior School		
	Bethan Roberts	26
	Louise Lynam	26
	Symon Bayley	27
	Sarah Williams	28
Briscoe Junior School		
	Christine Packman	28
	Kerry Strong	29
	Natalie Coote	29
	Kevin Dear	30
	Victoria Honeybul	30
	Tom Clinton	31
	Clair Morris	31
	Van Trinh	32
	Lisa Venables	32
	Nikki Pack	33
	Emma Goss	33

	Danny Shaw	34
	Samantha Lilley	34
Burnham CP School		
	Emma Coombe	35
Chigwell CP School		
	Claire White	35
	Mark Mina	36
	Madeleine Swan	36
Chipping Ongar Primary School		
	Lindsay Cousins	37
	Claire Fitzpatrick	38
College St Pierre		
	Katie Saunders	38
	Ross McGarrigle	39
	Alexander Lazell	40
Danbury Park CP School		
	James Mummery	40
	Laura Edmans	41
	Sophie Webber	41
	Jonathan Death	42
	Thomas Campion	42
	Yetti Arnold	43
	James Brown	43
	Jennifer Proudfoot	44
	Ian Kingsford	44
	Claire Best	44
	Gregory Foster	45
Earls Colne GM Primary School		
	Claire Moles	45
	Tom McCubbine	46
	Emma Starckey	46
	Emma Ivatt	47
	Elizabeth Hayes	47
	Michaela McCarthy	48
	Lucy Fryer	48
	Jodie Graham	49
	Danielle Weston	49
	Elizabeth Gill	50

	Steven Ling	50
	Jessica Burnup	51
	David Mann	51
	Katie Cooper	52
	Victoria Boyling	52
	Luke Lazaro	53
	Roxanne O'Brien	53
	Gillian Trask	54
	Mark Dawson	54
Earls Hall Junior School		
	Marc Sowerbutts	55
	Hannah Jacobs	55
	Hannah Drury	56
	Louise Woods	56
	Katie Walker	57
	Sebastian Miller	57
	Jeanette Brennan	58
	Genine Miles	58
	Hannah L Davies	59
	Emily Winckless	60
	Hayley Jarvis	60
	Sonia Nisbet	61
	Daniel Kenton	61
	David Spencer	62
	Emma Derbridge	63
	Ayesha Zaher	64
	Naomi Gooch	64
	Katy Roper	65
	Rachel Louise Charman	65
	Francesca Chambers	66
	Alexandra Moyes	66
	Lauren McLeod	67
	Steven Crick	67
	Cecillia Makonyola	68
	Jennifer Martinali	69
Epping Upland CE Primary School		
	Hollie Bernardo	69
	Kimberley Freeman	70

	Sarah Skinner	70
	Andrew Hanson	71
Fairhouse Junior School		
	Sarah Gunning	71
	Louise Peck	72
	Rosanne Davison	72
	Callum Finn	73
Gascoigne Junior School		
	Peu Lamm Cheung	73
	Abby Gibson	74
Grafton Junior School		
	Sally Thwaites	74
	Danielle Leaver	75
	Adrian Brown	75
	Christopher Conway	76
	Natalie Smith	76
	Danielle Caton	77
	Brian Martin	77
	Natalie Garrett	78
	Lisa Davie	78
	Danielle Webb	79
	Michelle Barry	79
	Lauren Brown	80
	Stewart Gamage	80
	Craig Sullivan	81
	Sarah Chance	81
	Lee Cable	82
	Marc Grayston	82
Grove Junior School		
	Samantha Chase	83
	Eleanor Clarke	83
	Sara Lewis	84
	Lucy Hockey	85
	Anthony Risidore	85
	Katherine Lattaway	86
	Sarah Wotherspoon	86
	Ashley Perkins	87
	Kate Alderton	87

	Lucy Bowhay	88
	Helen Harris	88
	Charlotte Ford	89
	Marie Turner	89
	Adam Williams	90
	Graeme Roberts	90
	Charlene Hoy	91
Highwoods Primary School		
	Kerry O'Brine	91
Holly Trees County Junior School		
	Nikki Kemzura	92
	Catherine Woodman	92
	Ashley Pretlove	93
	Ceri Roberts	93
Holt Farm County Junior School		
	Natalie May Osburn	94
	Judy Law	94
	Laura E Deaves	95
	Kellie Louise Osburn	95
	Lindsey Hayward	96
John Bunyan Junior School		
	Jenny Dent	96
	Danny Hankin	97
	Vicky Sayward	97
	Liam Baker	98
	Michael Leipper	98
	Natalie Crysell	99
	Katy Mott	99
Kingston CP School		
	Lianne Roberts	100
	Victor McNeely	100
Lawford C of E School		
	Shaun Lock	101
	Chloe Read	101
	Adam Smith	102
	Mark Mills	102
	Douglas Fryer	102
	Victoria Brooks	103

Hannah Pratt	103
Danielle Springett	103
Louise Appleby	104
Daniel Chamberlain	104
Jonathan Taylor	105
Mark Thurlow	105
Piia Jeffries	106
Claire Appleby	106
Alexea Williams	107
Mark Kemp	107
Elizabeth Percival	108
Sarah McLachlan	108
Mark Munt	109
Maria Leonard	109
Zoë Clark	110
David Wright	110
Sarah Parker	111
Emma Page	111
Robert Abbott	112
Rhian Barrick	112
Kayleigh Toner	113
Louie Nutt	114
Laura Louise Gentry	114

Lincewood Junior School

Adam Monahan	115
Katie Louise Cooper	115
Rebekah Brewster	116
Georgie Baker	116
Michelle Iveson	116
Luke Wyatt	117
Alison Jackson	117
Sean Hogan	118
Victoria Aley	118
Heather Ilesley	119
Jennifer Clark	119
Verity Sullivan	120
Lisa Jackson	120
Amy Copping	121

Maldon Court School

Grace Theobld 121
Alison Payne 122
Catherine Pope 123
Robin Watkins 124

Plumberow Primary School

Laura Patience 124
Lauren Pang 125
David Reid 126
Jennifer Stratford 127
Jody Lacey 127
Lisa Candler 128
Daniel Bacon 128
Chris Jude 129
Michael Fuller 129
David Wederell 130
Hannah Welhelmy 131
James Michael 132
Simon Darby 132
Lara Docking 133
Emma Bagshaw 133
Michelle Frampton 134
Sophie Adams 134
Katie Smith 135
Paul Raven 135
Aaron Webb 136
David Sains 136
James Irvine 137

Quilters Junior School

Mary Boursnell 138
Amy Fraser 138
Natalie Moody 139
Naomi Embury 140
Anita Gupta 141
Alison Bateman 142

St Alban's RC JMI School, Hornchurch

Fiona McCluskey 143
Yvonne West 143

Sarah Fissler	144
James Willoughby	144
Danny Franklin	145
Ross Francis	145
Laura Osborn	146
Mary Munson	146
Billy Calvert	147
Tony Humphreys	147
Lucy Cannon	148
Charlotte Thacker	148
Daniel Kelly	149
Alex Campbell	149
Mark O'Connell	150
Lindsay Madden	150
Patrick Cannon	151
Louise Meehan	151
Ciara Honeyball	152
Lauren Eames	152
Kevin Quinlan	153
Liam Tegart	153
Caroline Upward	154

St Antony's RC School, Woodford Green

Anthony McShea	154
Lucy Morgan	155
Laura Parkinson	155
Lucy-Ann Wartnaby	156
Shanthini Crusz	156
Catherine Mahon	157

St Hilda's School, Westcliffe-on-Sea

Hannah Ryder	158
Jessica Lucey	159
Sophie Hunt	160
Katharine Davies	161
Lara Cardosi	161
Amy Tetchner	162
Victoria Hamme	162
Sarah Parmenter	163
Amy Cockell	164

Hollie Bunker	165
Laura Hurley	165
Hannah Sheridan	166

St Joseph the Worker RC Primary School, Hutton

Leanne Linwood	166
Max Ward	167
Hannah Harrison-Griffiths	168
Nicole Vella	168
Jack Maloney	169
Helen Davey	169
Mary-Louise Smith	170
Lucy Turnball	170
Ciaran Kehoe	171
Matthew Hooper	171

St Lawrence School, Rowhedge

Andrew Haswell	172
Lee Saunders	172
Sophie Fincham	173
Adam Thrower	173
Ian Vickery	174
Dale Young	174

St Luke's RC Primary School, Harlow

Philomena Loughran	175
Vanessa Lewis	175
Nathanael Ozanne	175
Claire O'Connor	176
Matthew Jennings	176

St Mary's Prittlewell CE Primary School, Southend-on-Sea

Victoria Humphreys	177
Glenn Little	177
Joanna Duckworth	178
Dean Hanby	178
Sam Stone	179
Louise Hodder	179
Fay Leese	180
Daniel Lee Bishop	180
Lisa Jane Fowke	181

St Mary's RC Primary School, Tilbury
Ciaran Finn	181
Stephanie Kok	182
Charlotte Ager	182
Mary Mcpherson	183
Chantelle Samba	183

St Peter's CE Primary School, South Weald
Hannah Walker	184
Ross Nicholson	184
Adam Samuel	185
Chris Portou	185
Helen Richardson	186
Ann Platt	186
Claire Belson	187
Antony Lynn	188
Fiona Hornsby	188
Carl Harvey	189
Phillip Purvis	190

St Philomena's Prep School, Frinton-on-Sea
Ellie Toosi	190
Naomi Burgoyne	191
Alexander McNulty	192
Thomas Davies	192
Clare Mainstone	193
Fiona Bates	194
Sophie Williams	194
Matthew Tandy	195
James Skilling	195

St Thomas More RC GM Primary School, Saffron Walden
Alaric Green	196

Scargill Junior School
Terry Munns	197
Jemma Addinall	197
Carl Orriss	198
Amy Cook	198
Christopher Bottoms	198
Amy Cook	199
David Barber	199

Towers Junior School
Mark Townley	200
Laura McLeod	200
Christopher Ager	201

Westerings Primary School
Rebecca Aldham	201

Wentworth Primary School
Nicola Fry	202
Emma Stone	202
Jonathan Harbage	203
Nicola Hollingdale	204
Fiona MacDonald	204

Westminster Prep School
Louise Longhurst	205
Helen Hill	206
Kirsty Ferris	206

Woodford County High School
Georgina Privett	207

Writtle Junior School
Louisa McKenzie	208
Rebecca Garland	208
Thomas Gibb	209
Katrina Soderquest	210
Annalise Long	210

MOTHER

She is the best mother ever,
I would never replace her no never,
I love her very much,
She has a very lovely touch,
Without her I'd feel so numb,
Thanks for being a great mum.

Manjinder Dhillon (10)

THE OLD CASTLE

The old castle is old
It's spooky in the night-time
Even when it's light,
It's very very dusty.
Nobody ever cleans it
It's got a big tower
that's got a big clock.
It's got a moat round it
It's got a dungeon too
And in the dungeon is a
very friendly ghost
and how you get down
to the cellar is a mystery.
Now that is the end of my
        Poem
So goodbye for now
        bye-bye-bye

Jenny Addis (9) Arthur Bugler Junior School

MY MUM

There's a very special lady in my life,
She makes me lunch and she makes me tea,
And she cares for me,
She cuddles me when I am sad
But she never goes mad
She loves me lots
Especially when I have spots
But the best thing about her is
She's my mum.

Jade Ahmed (9) Arthur Bugler Junior School

MY SCATTY KITTEN

He wears white socks,
He chases my feet,
He comes up in the
Morning when I am
asleep.

He cries for food,
And rubs round your
Leg
Then spends half an
hour tucked up in
Bed.

I love him lots
He is soft and sweet.
He thinks he is a
Tiger big and strong
But he is my little
kitten.

Leanne Petitt (9) Arthur Bugler Junior School

THE POOR BIRD

Stuck in that air tube not in my nest,
They're very weak with hardly feathers on my chest.
I began to wail calling to my mother,
And it seemed to me as if she wouldn't bother.
Then warm human hands brought me out,
Then I really began to shout.
I was put on some grass feeling very sad,
And I knew my mother would be really mad.
For I was not with her and the rest of my family,
I was there shivering very unhappily.
I realised I couldn't live anymore,
And I found myself by a back door.
I was sad and began to cry,
I didn't like the thought of going to die.
But then my mother came and gave me food,
And then I was in a good mood.
She kept coming, I got better and began to grow,
And I kept thinking I will live I just know.
I now am older and can fly,

And I am living and not going to die.

Victoria Bienvenu (9) Arthur Bugler Junior School

LIGHT

Starlight, moonlight
Bright bright sunlight
Glowing, gleaming, twinkling
Sparkling colourful
Coloured rainbows
Flashing lighting, shiny white
Stars, starlight, shiny white.

Jemma Gale (9) Arthur Bugler Junior School

THE SEA

The sea was cold
People were playing
in the sea, it was cold.
The sun was shining
on the sea.

Laura Hutchinson (9) Arthur Bugler Junior School

MUM

My mum is nice
She likes sugar and spice
I care about her a lot.
She's got lovely hair
A nice coat to wear
She's lovely to cuddle when I fall in a puddle.
I love my mum
She is good fun.
Her face is pretty as well.

Carly Merritt (8) Arthur Bugler Junior School

LOVING

I love a boy
He loves me
My friend is jealous because of me
I was playing a game, he came to me
My friend is jealous because of me
I'm dancing with him at the disco
My friend is jealous because of me.

Gemma Louise McGill (9) Arthur Bugler Junior School

FLORIDA FUN

Disney world is full of fun
Magical things for everyone
Water slides and scary rides
Fantasy acts as your guide
Mickey Mouse and Donald Duck
Cartoons bringing lots of luck
Excited children everywhere
Golden glows about their hair
Enchanted castle in the sky
Clouds of balloons floating high
Is Disney World really a dream
No it's there for all to be seen.

Georgia Weekes (8) Arthur Bugler Junior School

MY PONIES

I have five ponies
And their names are,
Buttons, Jade, Jem, Twinkle and Crystal
Buttons loves eating grass
And Crystal loves to be ridden
Jem and Twinkle fight each day
But I know they're only playing.
When I tack them up they try
to run away
When I ride them they're very fast
trotting, cantering, galloping
I put them in their stable
And then they go to sleep
And in the morning I let them graze
again.

Hayley Rawson (9) Arthur Bugler Junior School

MAN VERSUS MAN

Man versus Man
Not stopping wars but starting them,
The noise of a gun, fleeing people
Crying babies, screaming women,
Injured men, frightened children,
Dead bodies on the floor,
Humans running to the refugee camp,
Cattle at the cattle mart stampeding,
Help countries that are at war.

Man versus Man,
Hungry humans needing feeding,
Ground dusty, not fit to grow food,
Mankind not importing,
People starving and dying,
These are the conditions of the Third World.

James Hunter (9) Arthur Bugler Junior School

PORTRAIT OF A FRIEND

She has dark brown eyes
Really she does run fast
Always chattering to her best friend
Short brown hair
That touches her shoulders
Freckles on her face
In her dark green top
And her trousers
To her ankles
A really nice smile

Wendy Hickford (9) Arthur Bugler Junior School

PORTRAIT OF MY FRIEND

My friend's name is Jessica
She always makes me laugh
And she always cheers me up
She waits for me
And she always ties her hair back
And she's really very blond
And she's very tough with boys
And she likes me all times.

Samantha Mallia (9) Arthur Bugler Junior School

A PRICKLY PRICK

Leaves are on the ground
Dead pieces of twigs
If you touch a stick it will
give you a prick,
The trees are everywhere but
they are bare
So that shows that winter is
here
I go through the woods to look at
the trees
In the summer it's nice and bright
In winter it's dark as night
You never know when the winter will
be dead

Richard Hollington (9) Arthur Bugler Junior School

PORTRAIT ABOUT GARY

He thinks he's a hard nut
He thinks he knows everything
But he's good looking
with big blue eyes.
He thinks he's good at football
He's got a pony tail
He thinks he's cool
and he's got a girlfriend called Sam.
He is smaller to some people
And they can't stop talking
He wears glasses
He sleeps in boxer shorts
He's got a big nose
He likes building
and he chases the girls.

Joseph Galer (9) Arthur Bugler Junior School

WINTER IS

Winter is Jack Frost's palace.
Winter is red nose season with biting rain.
Winter is no pretty flowers just bare trees.
Winter is ice-skating on frozen lakes.
Winter is time for carols and woolly hats.
Winter is a brilliant time for sledging.
Winter is Christmassy-looking shops.
Winter is a brilliant ski-ing holiday.
Winter is a massive snowman in a dressing gown.
Winter is roast turkey and potatoes.

Christopher Straker (8) Bancroft's School, Preparatory Department

WINTER IS ...

Winter is a jolly time when lots of snow is here
Winter is a happy time and after we celebrate the New Year
Winter is cold ice biting you once and twice
Winter is the lovely time that Father Christmas comes
Winter is the time that owls sleep, tu-whit, tu-whoo,
Winter is the time of presents for you and me
Winter is the time that we always drink hot lime
Winter is the time of Christmas trees and no bumble bee
Winter is the time of year that we sing and cheer.

Nikki Walsh (8) Bancroft's School, Preparatory Department

THE MOON

Feet echo as they thump the ground,
Deathly silent like the grave,
Rutted ground like a race track,
Stuffy air that smells of death.
Egg shaped craters rough with tiny holes,
Jagged rock crumbles at a touch,
Infinite dry cracks, joined like a family tree.
Never-ending plains of uneven rock.
The air misty like a marsh without water.
I see a beautiful pinkie orange sunset on Earth,
Then I bound back to the ship and depart.

Jason Gerlis (10) Bancroft's School, Preparatory Department

THE FALCON

Her eyes, sharp and clear,
Looking for her victim.
Her ears, small but strong,
Listening for her victim.
Her nose, tiny but quiet,
Smelling for her victim.
Her feathers, pretty and delicate,
Camouflaging her from her victim.
Her tail, straight and plumed,
Lifting her from her victim.
Her wings, great and muscular,
Flying to her victim.
Her talons, cut powerfully,
Holding tightly to her victim.
Her beak, curved and clean,
Tearing at her victim.
Her stomach, broad and straining to fly,
Full, of her victim.

Jessica Charlesworth (10) Bancroft's School, Preparatory Department

THE BEE

Barrel shaped body with black and yellow stripes
Flying around collecting yellow pollen dust.
The pollen basket overflowing as it weaves its way
In and out of flowers.

The antennae bob up and down as they dance
about.
The wings too delicate to touch look like glass.
I'm always afraid when I go outside in bare feet
In case I tread on a bee.

Eleanor Lear (10) Bancroft's School, Preparatory Department

MOONSCAPE

Solid rock encircled me,
Disintegrating as I pick it up,
Remote black space
Expanding before my eyes,
As mist hangs upon the moon,
Blinding me,
As an American flag sways from side to side.

Sandipan Bhowmik (9) Bancroft's School, Preparatory Department

IS THAT ME?

Is that boy in the photograph me?
Wearing a hat and coat,
Standing beside some trees.
Was I so thin?
Was I so small?
He looks so sad I don't know him at all.
Who took the picture?
I think I was three or so.
I have almost forgotten,
But now it is familiar.
Those eyes like my mother,
And hair like my father,
He really is me!
That small, skinny boy,
Standing beside some trees.
But now I am older and
As I reminisce,
I feel quite regretful looking at this.

Saul Dindol (11) Bancroft's School, Preparatory Department

WHAT IS LOVE?

Is love a golden ball falling out of a hand?
A scarlet rose petal floating in the wind?
Is love a crispy leaf on the crumbling road?
A soft patch of warm white fur shrouding a kitten?
Is love a rainbow scattering colours here and there?
A sheep lost in a field abandoned and lonely?
Is love the incessant pain we feel in our bleeding hearts?
A bar of chocolate melting on our tongue?
Is love the warmth of a blazing fire?
A golden trophy standing proudly on a shelf?
Is love the water from the salt blue and foamy sea?
An echo of a droning voice, calling far away?
Or is love a caring family ready to smile at you?
We all know what love is but do others?

Shama Naqushbandi (11) Bancroft's School, Preparatory Department

IS THAT ME?

Is that me in that photo?
Screaming and bawling at my brother,
Strapped into my high chair.

Is that me in that photo?
Struggling to be free,
To run like my brother.

Is that me in that photo?
Tear-stained face and fine, dishevelled mousy hair.
Who would recognise me now?

Is that me in that photo?
Shouting at my parents
'Get rid of my brother'

Is that me in that photo?
A little toddler of one,
Wanting to be free.

That is me,
The girl who had and still has,
That aggravating big brother!

Victoria Wojewodka (11) Bancroft's School, Preparatory Department

AUNT ETHEL

Aunt Ethel is my favourite aunt,
She has eyes as blue as the ocean,
Tresses and tresses of golden hair,
Her voice as soft as snowfall.

Aunt Ethel is my favourite aunt,
She's always busy doing something,
She's a humorous and sociable lady,
And her favourite past-time is shopping!

Aunt Ethel is my favourite aunt,
She loves collecting vases,
She has a husband called Edgar,
And she always attends her aerobic classes!

Aunt Ethel is my favourite aunt,
She loves cooking roast dinners,
Whenever I go to visit her,
She cooks one just for me!

Anna Maddox (11) Bancroft's School, Preparatory Department

THE SUN

The sun's shining
So brightly
I am burning.
We've got a black car
that does not help a lot
My body's brown
My legs are red
I've got hay fever
That does not help ever
Achoooocoo
And we are driving in this long
Black car for a very long time.
I am sweating like a pig
in the back here
I'm bored
I want an ice-cream
I want a drink
Mum, I start
Then I saw it the blazing sunlight
There it is, our destiny.

Ruth Boatwright (9) Beckers Green School

SNOW

Snow, flaky cold, snowflakes on
the ground, iced ponds, snowmen with
top hats, snowflakes on the ground,
Snow fights, soft snowflakes, snowflakes
on the ground, soon it is spring.

Sean Mark Attwood (9) Beckers Green School

THUNDER

In the middle of the night,
I turn on my bedroom light.
I hear a great flash,
They come together and they smash.
It looks powerful and bright,
It shines in the middle of the night.
Lightning is very bright,
Shining in the frosty night.
Thunder sparkles and flashes,
Lightning is not very frightening.
When they get near they make
a wonderful flash.
I'm not scared of lightning but thunder
is very frightening.
Thunder is horrible and terrible,
very scary, I hate thunder.

Larnce Forrester (9) Beckers Green School

RAIN

Rain is wet, rain is fun, I splash
in the daytime, it sure
is fun when the rain comes
down you see hundreds of
little rain drops.
It's a really hot day and it's
raining, the rain is rattling against
the windows.
Mum opens all the windows
and I get wet.

Oh Mum!

Elener Ambrose (9) Beckers Green School

THUNDER

Thunder crashes
Sometimes it's fun laying on my bed
thinking there's someone coming to get me.
'Mum' I yell
Oh, don't be silly
There's nothing there.

SUN

I like the sun, that's not scary,
It's hot but I don't mind,
      up high burning in the sky
The sun's my friend.

RAIN

I like rain
It's lovely weather for me
And the ducks

Serena Dunne (9) Beckers Green School

SUMMER

S unny weather I love
U mbrellas I don't need
M um says don't forget your sun hat
M um I say is this one alright.
E veryone is hot but I am
R eally really hot.

Charlotte Twaites (9) Beckers Green School

THUNDER

I don't like Thunder, it's scary loud Bang
goes the Thunder. I don't like rain
when it Thunders it makes me more
scared.
I don't like Thunder, it's scary
I don't like Thunder and I never will.

Nikki Clark (9)   Beckers Green School

RAIN

Rain is boring
As it's pouring
Is it stopping?
No it's still raining
I am bored when it's pouring
Now it is stopping
Good I can go out!

Tony Robert Hardy (9)   Beckers Green School

STORM

It's getting windy.
Soon clouds will be in the sky.
They will be black clouds
Soon I will have to go and hide.
Oh no! I can hear thunder crackling
Soon it will be pouring down with rain.
Ahhhh! I am getting soaked
I'd better go and hide.

Kate Coxell (9)   Beckers Green School

LIGHTNING

Thunder and Lightning, very very frightening.
And Lightning, Lightning never never
frightening because Lightning is not very
frightening. Thunder is very very
frightening because Lightning is not always
frightening so Lightning Lightning never
never frightening. Frightening never
never Lightning.

Leah Ashdown (9) Beckers Green School

THE SUN

Big sun
Hot sun
Very hard to reach sun
Hot sun
Big sun
Always just a hot sun

Big sun
Hot sun
Such a big strong sun
Big sun
Hot sun
Always such a big sun

Hot sun
Big sun
Very hot and sticky.
Big sun
Hot sun
Always just the same sun

Charlotte West (9) Beckers Green School

MY FISH

Small and slippery
Delicate and docile
And he's rather greedy.
He darts around like a bullet
When you go and feed him.

Emma Catterall (10) Beehive Lane CP School

THE SPECKLED SHELL

Static on a radio
tadpoles in milk
smooth as a pearl
jagged like a cliff
catacombs leading to a deep dark cave
stalactites hanging from the ceiling
like pointed teeth

Roy Clancy (10) Beehive Lane CP School

THE STARRY NIGHT

Looks like a sad picture.
balls of fire
like marbles.
Yellow stars light up the sky.
Flying saucers
exploding bombs.
Sky looks like a fiasco,
looks like sea splashing.
Tornado coming from the West.

Louise Swinney (10) Beehive Lane CP School

THE FOOTBALLER

Kick the ball around in the dust
Ball juggling on his feet and his head.
Eight children squashed in one bed.
He dreamt that he would play for
Argentina and win the world cup for
them.
Diego made it and he became rich he
scored one of the best goals in the
world.
He threw it away by taking cocaine
He ruined his career and now it's all
over
And he's thirty four
and he's got nothing.

Adam Brewster (10) Beehive Lane CP School

THE FEEL OF FROST

Tingling fingers,
Aching toes,
Freezing ears,
And a bright red nose.
Frost is on the window pane,
My toes have frozen (not
again)
Cold shivers running down my
spine,
To be indoors would be just
fine.

Jennifer Mack (10) Beehive Lane CP School

THE CELEBRATIONS ON VE DAY

Now the war is over,
We can live our lives again,
The celebrations, street parties,
The war has come to an end.
No more bombs flying,
And no more planes.
Now the war is over,
We can live our lives again.

Matthew Fowler (11) Blenheim CP School

WATER

Pitter, Patter,
Pitter, Pitter, Patter.
The rain whispered and shouted at the same time,

As it hit the window pane with tremendous power,
And exploded into millions of droplets
Bursting everywhere.

I see two head lamps of a car
And hear the humming,
As dad skids in the drive.

The rain takes over.

Pitter, Patter,
Pitter, Pitter, Patter.
The rain whispered and shouted at the same time.

Richard Woolener (9) Boxted C of E Primary School

FOG

Fog feeling moist
on my face.
When it clears it is
damp on the grass.
And wet soggy
leaves,
Drip with dew from
the fog.

James Brooks (9) Boxted C of E Primary School

THE WATERFALL

Tumbling, chattering down the slope,
Between lush banks of green,
As great and tall a waterfall,
As ever has been seen,
The bubbling rapids laugh and chase,
Among rocks fringed with white foam lace,
All long white ropes of swirling foam,
Each one is every other's clone,
Falling swift with rushing grace,
From swirling heights to foaming base,
Over it the spruce trees lean,
Of pale, or dark, or browny green.
Steep banks of clay on either side,
Red clay sweeps down in a gentle glide,
On every side the trees stand tall,
Beside the rushing waterfall.

Dora Steel (9) Boxted C of E Primary School

OUT OF THE NIGHT

You dance by dusky water,
You haunt along the stream,
You wait until the bat squeaks from the sky,
You slip in through my window
As secretly as a dream,
You stealthily approach where I lie.

You're delicate and dainty,
Your song though faint is fine,
Your limbs are long and very slender too,
Your touch at first is gentle,
But really must you dine
On me, mosquito, I would not on you.

Paul Wiggins (10) Boys' High School, Colchester

MY CAT

My cat Jesse with his green
and yellow eyes
comforts me when I'm sad.
My cat Jesse with his black
and white fur
often likes to purr.
My cat Jesse is sometimes bad
and often acts a little mad.
Climbing trees is his favourite game
and often leads him into shame.
For once a tree he did climb
and there he spent a very long time.

And this ends my very long rhyme

James Maxfield (10) Boys' High School, Colchester

ZAC THE CAT

Zac the playful cat.
Who jumps from bed to bed.
He hides and waits to pounce on his prey
Oh, that playful cat
He runs from room to room.
Hoping for a game with his friends.
He eats their food.
He sits by the sink watching the bubbles pop.
Oh, that playful cat.
He chases a fly up the curtains and falls onto the floor.
He's back again for some more.
Oh, that playful cat.
Now it's all quiet, where is he?
Laying in the sunshine fast asleep, until the next time.
Oh, that playful cat.

Mark Stobbs (9) Boys' High School, Colchester

THUMPER

My rabbit is called Thumper
She is very greedy
Her coat is like a jumper
For food she's always needy
If she gets any plumper
She won't fit in her cage.

Ben Russell (10) Boys' High School, Colchester

MY CAT LEO

My cat Leo,
He's all mine,
He's playful,
But cheerful,
He's never a grouch.
He's rather a soft cat,
But never looks it,
Because he's so alert,
And when I go up to him,
He knows attention's here.

Tim France (10) Boys' High School, Colchester

BIMBO

She is fluffy
People say she looks like a bear
She comforts my cat
She loves me
She is not rough with my friends
She is cute
Everyone loves her
       Because she is my dog.

Tobias Larsen (10) Boys' High School, Colchester

ANIMALS IN SPRING

Springtime, springtime
lovely lovely
birds are singing.
Hibernation's over
Hooray hooray
Out come the animals
one, two, three
Big and small animals
Ugly animals
Pretty animals
They're all so beautiful
I don't want hibernation
to come again.

Bethan Roberts (9) Brightside Junior School

UNDER WATER

I dive into the deep dark blue sea
I go deep down
To the depths of the sea.
I see lots of friendly animals
Splashing dolphins
Coloured fish
Great big sharks
Suddenly I see this strange big grey shape
I go closer, closer
The big shape is a Great White Shark!
I go closer, closer, to see if it is friendly
but it chases after me.
So I swim and swim
but I can't get away
So I'm inside.

Louise Lynam (9) Brightside Junior School

I WISH I WAS A FISH

They swim in the ocean
They swim in the sea
They've got so much freedom
Oh how happy I'd be

Their coats are all shiny
They glitter and gleam
They are so very happy
Or so they all seem

They show all the people
The things they can do
You may even find some
Swimming in the zoo.

All day they can wander
They glide to and fro
If they swim a long time
They'll give a little blow
In all of my dreams
There's cool water round me
I'd swim the Seven Seas
A fish, I wish, I could be.

Symon Bayley (9) Brightside Junior School

THE MOOR

Looking out of the window at my tiny little garden
But I have a better garden, a much much better garden,
it is a wonderful moor.
It is a beautiful moor with heather everywhere, the
trees are full of colourful leaves, there are buttercups
all around me.
When it is windy the trees are wild, the buttercups
bobbing and swaying.
When it is rainy I go down to the moor, I feel
so bored because I can't run, jump and play.
I look up at the sky and watch the rain as it turns
into streams, the streams turn into rivers, and the
rivers go down to the seas.
When it is spring there is blossom on the trees, and
when it falls down it is like a thick carpet.
This moor I am trying to describe to you.
But I really can't. I wish I could take you
there but I could not, because that wonderful moor,
that beautiful moor is just in my mind.

Sarah Williams (8) Brightside Junior School

WAR

First trapped in a van,
Then taken away from my parents,
I felt like reaching out for them.
Now electric fences everywhere.
I see people go into gas chambers.
Cries of terrified children.
Cries of hunger and fear.

Christine Packman (10) Briscoe Junior School

HOLOCAUST

Terrified children
Standing behind
barbed wire
Crying helplessly inside
Clothes all ragged
and torn
dirty from no washing
Faces go thin
from no food
Their minds going blank
from everything but fear
and death
Just knowing you were
going to get gassed
any day
Your life going out
Like a candle
burning down.

Kerry Strong (10) Briscoe Junior School

FLOWERS

Big flowers, little flowers,
All in a heap.
Getting ready to reap.
They sing in spring.
And dance in the summer time
Singing their little summer rhyme.

Natalie Coote (9) Briscoe Junior School

HOLOCAUST

Trapped no way out.
Barbed wire surrounded everyone.
Terrified faces.
Silent screams of unhappiness.
Children's clothes ragged.
Thin scared children.
hungry cold people
people scraping feet.
Wagons up and down the tracks.
Never-ending lines
people in and out of wagons
one way work
one way death.

Kevin Dear (10) Briscoe Junior School

IF I WAS ANNE BOLEYN

If I was Anne Boleyn
It would be fab.
I would make funny faces at everybody
And my daughter Elizabeth
Will be ill after lots of fights
So be mates forever and
Care for Henry the VIII and
All the other Tudor people
And don't chop heads off
Like they did. OK!

Victoria Honeybul (9) Briscoe Junior School

HOLOCAUST

My friends and family are gone
I'm working just to drag dead bodies
to strip them
and to burn them
Just to help, to help the Germans
to help them!
I shouldn't be here
I should be at home
at home with my family
My family are dead
It's like being sucked into a pit of
dark hopelessness
with no-one around
It's terrible, just terrible, I'm going
to die
I throw my shoe at the barbed wire
fence
A surge of electricity runs through it
I throw myself at the fence!

Tom Clinton (11) Briscoe Junior School

BIRDS

Flying high in the sky *Birds*.
Way up there in the air fly *Birds*.
Swooping! Looping! Soaring!
Diving fly *Birds*.
Eating bread fluttering down *Birds*.
Fluttering swooping! Soaring! Looping! *Birds*.

Clair Morris (9) Briscoe Junior School

LONELINESS

Lonely almost every day,
On the wall with nothing to do,
Nobody wants to play with me,
Even all my friends.
Like feeling I'm invisible,
You may not see me at all.
Nobody likes me anymore.
Everywhere I go
Seeing people happy
Playing a friendly game
Or playing a joke

Van Trinh (9) Briscoe Junior School

WHY WERE THE GERMANS SO CRUEL?

Terrified as I go into the pitch black wagon
The six hour journey was too much for people
Suffocating with children. My life torn away by
emptiness and darkness
No room
No air
No life for me to live separated from my parents
Children crying with no food to eat, people trapped in
Shame and fright, old people trapped on barbed wire
Concentration camps with coldness and hunger and
going in to be gassed ten minutes later silent
and still. Smell of bodies being burnt
People in a line fit or not fit to work
All their belongings in a line as they tremble with fear.
People lighting candles on the railway track,
There's no life for them anymore.

Lisa Venables (10) Briscoe Junior School

WINTER

It's winter it's cold
Stay indoors to play.

You can play cars
Or you can play board games

As long as you have got toys
You shouldn't be bored

And when the winter's over
You can go and play football

Or go and play 'had'
And then I hope you won't
be sad.

Nikki Pack (9) Briscoe Junior School

IN THE PLAYGROUND

Miss!
Miss!
She did that,
he did this,
he hit me,
she pushed me,
and she hit me.
Miss.
She's chasing me
and I said, 'No don't chase me!'
Miss!
Give this girl a yellow card.

Emma Goss (8) Briscoe Junior School

SUMMER TIME

It's beautiful. Indescribable red, green, cold.
The picture's so bold. Trees rustling and flowers are
tussling, to try and burst out of the ground.
And I would love to see them win.

Danny Shaw (9) Briscoe Junior School

WHAT WOULD MAKE A LOVELY ROAST DINNER

What would make a lovely
roast dinner is
slugs with mud and worms
spiders and cobwebs
with Yorkshire puds
with snails and a monkey's
tail.

Samantha Lilley (9) Briscoe Junior School

POLLUTION'S A SCARE

Pollution pollution is all
I can see,
How much pollution can
there be?

Pollution here,
Pollution there,
Too much pollution,
could be a scare.

Don't be stupid
do not pollute
that would not
be very cute.

The world would
be a better place
If we didn't pollute
now I rest my case.

Emma Coombe (11) Burnham CP School

SNAIL RACE

Down in the garden.
Where the white roses flower.
Summer is bringing.
Its own special power.
Two snails race.
Face to face.
Slowly crawling up the gate.
They came across a big ugly spider.
The spider's name was Hairy Myra.
And so the race is carrying on.
I turn around and then they're gone.

Claire White (10) Chigwell CP School

COMPUTING

Mouses clicking,
Time bombs ticking,
Virus infecting,
Anti virus disinfecting,
It's all happening in your computer.

Colours flashing,
Screen scrolling,
Sprites moving,
Joypad pressing,
It's all happening in your computer.

Floppy disks entering,
Floppy disks exiting,
Programs loading,
Games loading,
Swapping disks,
Don't have to with ROM discs,
It's all happening in your computer.

Mark Mina (10) Chigwell CP School

NONSENSE

If a friend is someone you like
and an enemy is someone you hate,
What is a frenemy?

And if you eat with your mouth
and hear with your ears,
What would you do with a mear?

And if beer tastes bitter
and chocolate tastes sweet,
What does bocolate taste like?

And if drink is a liquid
and food is a solid,
What is drood?

And if this poem isn't Mike's
and if this poem isn't Jane's
It must be mine!

Madeleine Swan (10) Chigwell CP School

GARDENS

My garden is a nice place,
Very neat and lots of space
It is a place where I have fun
And play with my rabbits in the run.
I have a patch of my very own
Where seeds for pretty flowers are grown.
I like it when it is very hot,
When I put my pool in a shady spot.
In winter too it is very nice,
As I play in the snow and slide on ice,
But my garden is the best in spring,
When the plants all bud and the birds all sing.

Lindsay Cousins (8) Chipping Ongar Primary School

GIFTS

A gift is a kiss

    A gift is a cuddle

        A gift is being kind

A gift is being loving

    A gift is lots of things in a
        different way.

Claire Fitzpatrick (8) Chipping Ongar Primary School

ANIMALS

Animals are nice,
Animals are cuddly.
Animals I have six of them.
Animals are kind.
Animals are the best.

The reason why I like them,
Is because they are loving and true.
And they are my best friends,
Because they are kind to my family
too.

Katie Saunders (8) College St Pierre

COLOURS

Blue is for sky,
Red is for fire,
Green is grass,
Black is for tyre,
Pipes are sometimes brass.
Orange is for pumpkin,
Brown is for wood
Grey is for pavement
Mum calls me in but I don't think I should.
It might be for tidying up *Oh No!*
Hey wait a minute it might be good.

Yellow is for sun,
Purple is for flower,
Amber is for traffic lights,
Mr Muscle has got power.
Violet is for crayon,
Pink is for skin,
Gold is for money,
England always win.
The sky goes black,
It's time for bed,
Another adventure to play with Fred.

Ross McGarrigle (8) College St Pierre

COLOURS

Some colours are beautiful,
What would we do without them?
Colours are wonderful,
How would things look without them?
The green and brown on the trees in the forest,
Oh how would they look without them?
The lovely red roses,
Oh how would we feel without them?
We are really lucky to have colours,
Because how would things look without them?

Alexander Lazell (9) College St Pierre

WIND

Wind blowing great oak
trees to the ground.
Using its strong power to smash
homes and buildings into rubble.
This amazing power is being captured
by the spinning blades of towering windmills
Being changed into electricity energy for all.

James Mummery (11) Danbury Park CP School

THE NEVER-ENDING POLES

The endless obtrusive poles reaching for the clouds in the sky.
The sharp blades loop, twist and turn at the top of the never-ending poles.
Out in the countryside or in the sea these unsightly things lie.
The refreshing wind curls and whistles in the air
Then the blustery winds come rushing through the swirling blades.

Laura Edmans (10) Danbury Park CP School

OUR POWERFUL WATCHERS

Wind turbines looming bright
Standing high and tall, modernised towers.
Watching the country's every move.
Looming spikes tower above a landscape of cowering grass.
Modernised metal standing behind a backdrop of living life.
A whirlwind of power blowing a gale
Around the white, bright skyscrapers.
Spacious knives rotating round again, again.
Making noise they will shout
Twirling, coiling, looping, whirling
Over and over until the wind dies.

Sophie Webber (10) Danbury Park CP School

THE FOUR SEASONS

Spring is . . .
Pink and white ovals floating down.
Big white eggs hatching open.
Yellow trumpets swaying in the breeze.
Chocolate eggs being swallowed up.

Summer is . . .
Velvet bees collecting sweet sticky nectar.
Golden sunlight flooding down.
Swimming in the deep blue sea.
Green grass and beautiful flowers covering the hillside.

Autumn is . . .
Colourful leaves dropping from trees
Like petals from a dying flower.
Harvest festivals ringing out.
Fierce conker fights raging around.
Fruits falling from the great old trees
Gratefully eaten by wasps.

Winter is . . .
Whitened landscapes rolling away like a big white sheet.
Wrapping paper being ripped to shreds like recycled paper.
Snowballs thrown from place to place.
Icy knives stabbing into me.

Jonathan Death (9) Danbury Park CP School

THE BUSY BEE'S DAY

I heard a noise, it sounded like a hungry dragon.
The sky was blue the sun was high, hot sizzling and fiery
I heard a bee trying to get some pollen.

Thomas Campion (9) Danbury Park CP School

LET ME HAVE SOME

The iced-gem looks small and round,
Twirled pink, with white, yellow and brown.
Flat and lovely it looks tasty and gorgeous.
It makes me mutter to myself.
It smells sweet and juicy,
Tasting cold, hard, powdery and crispy.
Hard, icy biscuit
Lemon and strawberry.
    Yum!

Yetti Arnold (10) Danbury Park CP School

THE AMAZING YORKSHIRE PUDDING

Crispy, golden Yorkshire puddings,
Resting amazingly on the china plate.

The delightful, circular inflated food,
Coming out of the steaming oven.

The fresh, delicious smell of the pudding,
Is dragging me to the plastic tray,
Where it is laying.

The tasty, wonderful Yorkshire puddings,
Making my tongue wrap around my lips.

The relaxing taste of the squidgy outside,
Feeling like foam inside my watering mouth.

The extraordinary, delicious taste,
Is best with a smooth mint sauce.

James Brown (10) Danbury Park CP School

URANIUM

*U*ranium is dangerous,
*R*eactors are vital.
*A*lways a little bit of trouble,
*N*ever used in the wrong way when it is buried.
*I*t is buried in a lead box.
*U*ranium *Beware.*
*M*en have to wear heavy suits in the reactor.

Jennifer Proudfoot (9) Danbury Park CP School

THE TWISTING SHARP BLADES

The blades look sharp and prickly with a bean pole underneath,
They could cut anything.
The turbines in the sea look like a deserted island, with twisting wings.
The wind can be blustery, draughty and like a whirlpool
Never stopping until the whirlpool dies down and the turbines are finished
Until the blades start twisting, spinning, looping and whirling again.

Ian Kingsford (10) Danbury Park CP School

THE TALL TURBINE

The turbine is a tall, long pole with an amazing white propeller.
The turbine stands in the stormy, blue sea where the rough wind blows.
The wind blows, the wind departs,
The turbine gets slower, but does not stop completely.
It reminds me of the bumpy waves in the rough, blue sea.

Claire Best (9) Danbury Park CP School

HOLLY LEAVES

The leaves look like a dark green dragon.
The leaves feel like a stinging nettle.
The leaves look like shiny paper.
The stem is wrought and it looks like lots of little hills.
The berry reminds me of red sweets and red juicy apples.

Gregory Foster (10) Danbury Park CP School

EXPERTS

I know someone who can do
ten cartwheels in ten seconds

I know someone who is
good at art work and painting

I know someone who can
write their name with their toes

I know someone who can
eat a piece of bread in seconds

I know someone who can
hold twenty snails on her hands

I know someone who can
ride her bike with no hands

I know someone who can
ride a horse in a circle without falling off

And that someone is . . . *Me!*

Claire Moles (9) Earls Colne GM Primary School

THE 1930'S

Sooty buildings up to the sky.
Houses covered in grime,
Pitch black streets.
Down in the alley,
Stray cats move.
Fog, thicker than stone,
Tickles your face
Dull coloured people
Walk the streets
Children collect firewood
The 1930's were a bad time.

Tom McCubbine (9) Earls Colne GM Primary School

A DIRTY LIFE

Dull and misty
On a gloomy cold night
The thick fog follows
Unhappy people along
The murky streets
Our houses are covered
In pitch black dirt
Caused by the fumes
From the factories.

Emma Starckey (9) Earls Colne GM Primary School

THE 1930'S

As I walk out of my door
The thick fog feels like
Cold hands around my face
I can't see
I wander down the
Deserted streets
Rummaging in dustbins
To find wood for a fire
I don't find any and
It's a long journey home
On the way I see
The men marching down
To London.

Emma Ivatt (10) Earls Colne GM Primary School

FOGGY DAY

On this misty foggy day
Dark streets turn a
Sunless day into a
Gloomy night
People scrape for food
In tattered clothes
Steel tipped clogs
Flat checked caps and
Scarves round their cold necks.

Elizabeth Hayes (10) Earls Colne GM Primary School

GRAVEYARDS

A sad lonely place
Scary and miserable
No-one goes there
It's much too frightening!
Great black gates I really hate
Trees like monsters
Waiting for their dinner
Church bells ringing slowly
As one ghost pulls the eight ropes
A soft distant voice
Singing sweetly. Soon
There will be a ghostly party.
A sad lonely place
Scary and miserable
The graveyard - no mistake.

Michaela McCarthy (10) Earls Colne GM Primary School

THE WOODS

The woods are a lovely place to be when
Nocturnal animals come out
Badger, deer, fox and bat
The woods are a lovely place to be when
In daylight branches rustle in the wind
Then dusk falls and all is quiet.

The woods are a lovely place to be when
Dawn breaks and birds sing
In the beautiful morning sky
The woods are a lovely place to be when
At midday animals come out to play and
Stoats chase rabbits.

Lucy Fryer (9) Earls Colne GM Primary School

HAIKU

Blossom falls from trees
fresh scent drifting towards us
bird song in the sky

Jodie Graham (10) Earls Colne GM Primary School

I CAN SMELL...

I can smell
A bad bad spell
Cast by the witch
Who puts in her cauldron:

> *Rats' eyeballs*
> *Cats' tails too*
> *Fish fins*
> *Human eyes*
> *Slimy rotten frogs' legs*
> *Bats' bones smooth and small*
> *Rotten flea eggs*
> *Cold tingling spider webs too*

And that's the end
Of her bad bad stew
Oh, she needs a finishing touch
And she's chosen

> *You!*

Danielle Weston (10) Earls Colne GM Primary School

MY FACE

My face - plum shaped
My eyes - crawling beetles
My nose - a pear in the middle of a fruit bowl
My ears - bats flying through the air
My skin - sandpaper rubbed on a wall
My eyebrows - a velvet dress trailing
My hair - soft lioness coat.

Elizabeth Gill (10) Earls Colne GM Primary School

THE BLITZ

The Blitz
The all clear sounds
The smell of burning rubble
The sound of people sobbing
A dog whines while
People clear the road
It's dark and wet
The fires are still burning
Round craters in the ground
The sky is full of smoke.
The droning of German bombers in the distance
Back to the shelter we go
The sound of bombs begins again.

Steven Ling (10) Earls Colne GM Primary School

THE BLITZ

The All Clear sounds
Outside, a dreadful creepy
Feeling sweeps over me.
One moment, bombs dropping.
The next
Silence.
I look around
My home
Nowhere to be seen.
Where will we stay?
The smell of burning rubble drives me crazy.
I hate it out here.
I dash back to the shelter.

Jessica Burnup (10) Earls Colne GM Primary School

VOLCANO

Boiling
Smoky
Steaming fire
Flowing down the side of a major volcano
Flowing into everything around.

David Mann (8) Earls Colne GM Primary School

FRAGRANCE

I love the smell of:

>perfumes on my wrist
>flowers in a meadow
>grass cut in a long summer
>air after the rain
>antiseptic sprayed on a rabbit hutch
>and
>leather shoes.

Katie Cooper (10) Earls Colne GM Primary School

EXPLOSION

The All Clear sounds!
It's night time and scary.
Smells of burning
Wood, rubber, clothes,
Flesh.
Dogs howl
Cats hiss
Children whimper
Digging to find trapped people.
Craters in the ground
Fires still burning
A policeman keeps
The crowd back.
Suddenly
The distant sound of planes throbbing
Back to the shelter again.

Victoria Boyling (10) Earls Colne GM Primary School

THE BLITZ

We hurried out of the shelter to find a sight
We never expected to see
Destroyed and derelict buildings
Dogs howling in the distance
People buried under the rubble
Fires still blazing
People searching, dodging
Falling bricks
Devastation everywhere.

Luke Lazaro (10) Earls Colne GM Primary School

WAR

With relief I hear the siren stop
I leave the shelter and the
Smell of burning rubber
Makes me shiver
I hear people crying
Fires crackling
Our house has vanished
Along with five others
I panic
Our cat was in there
I pick through the rubble
I sigh
No use - it's too deep!

Roxanne O'Brien (10) Earls Colne GM Primary School

BLITZ

I came out of the shelter
To totally different streets
I could smell fire, burning wood
People screaming, shouting, sprinting
Our house was destroyed
Bombed - a direct hit
A pile of rubble
Where would we live now?

Gillian Trask (10) Earls Colne GM Primary School

I HATE THIS WAR

The siren screams.
To the shelter I dash.
All around
A fluttering sound
Landmines!
On parachutes.
Suddenly - a giant explosion.
The target . . . I wonder . . .
The pub?
Or my home?
We lie waiting
For the all clear to sound.

Mark Dawson (10) Earls Colne GM Primary School

MIGHTY MARS GOD-OF-WAR

Marching loudly into action
Armour shining, blinding
Ready to kill is *Mars!*
Swords swing, swang - blood gushes

Gods - boom, crash, wallop
Over the sea of fighting soldiers
Dying warriors

Out came his shiny mighty sword
Fierce Gods wanting to win

War ends with a scattered army
At last the Gods destroyed
Romans are victorious.

Marc Sowerbutts (9) Earls Hall Junior School

MARS - THE GOD OF WAR

Trumpets playing
Drums drumming
Romans led out to battle
Warriors rushing to escape
Pandemonium!
Screaming and yelling
Tortured cries
Soldiers left dying
Among those who where already dead
Piercing javelins through shields and warriors
Pandemonium!
Chaos!
Evil!

Hannah Jacobs (9) Earls Hall Junior School

SPRING TIME

*S*pring is fun every day,
*P*laying round in a happy sort of way,
*R*unning round and picking flowers,
*I*sn't the sun shining for hours and hours,
*N*obody hates spring,
*G*oing places happiness it can bring,

*T*ogether people having fun,
I really, really love the sun,
*M*orning sunshine will very soon come
*E*aster eggs are very yum!

Hannah Drury (11) Earls Hall Junior School

I WOULD LIKE TO PAINT

I would like to paint the mind of a dog
when it barks away.

I would like to paint the dream of alligator
when the sunset falls over night

I would like to paint the thoughts of an
animal before being put down.

I would like to paint a unicorn flying high
over the moon.

I would like to paint a dream of an orphan
child who wants to go home.

I would like to paint the sky's deep blue colour
before the pollution of the factories smoke.

Louise Woods (10) Earls Hall Junior School

THE DEFEAT OF MARS

Storming!
Jumping!
Fighting!
Evil as a pack of wolves
Destroying homes,
Thundering!
All of a sudden a cloud of smoke
Gone!
People settled down
Five minutes later
A cloud of smoke again
This time with weapons
More powerful than before
With swords, spears, daggers
All throwing them at the same time
People dying in pain
Children, adults picked
Up and tortured
Bows and arrows shooting through
The air.

Katie Walker (8) Earls Hall Junior School

WINTER

Winter looming round the corner,
Waiting till autumn is dead,
And when it dies it pounces,
And kills everything in its stride.

Sebastian Miller (11) Earls Hall Junior School

I AM A ROSE

I am a rose, as red as your cheeks
I am as small as your feet, but as
beautiful as your garden, so please
don't tread on me as I don't make
a noise, please water me every day
and I will be as big as your legs,
I am here for everybody to enjoy,
So please let me stay as
your red rose . . .

Jeanette Brennan (10) Earls Hall Junior School

DOWN SHE GOES

Bang!
A big ice-berg hits the ship
People waking
Pandemonium!

I was as scared as a very scared hamster
Thrown into a life boat
Hearing people drown
Sadly the big ship went down
I survived thanks to my very lucky stars
but I knew it would always haunt me
It would always haunt me.

Genine Miles (9) Earls Hall Junior School

I SHOULD LIKE TO PAINT

I should like to paint
The glistening of the snow
As the morning sun beams down
And capture the brightness of the sun's rays

I would like to paint
The sound of the snow
Crunching beneath my feet
And its coldness in my fingers

I would like to paint
The ice cracking in the coldness
Or the roaring of a polar bear
While pouncing on its prey

I should like to paint the sound of the seagulls
Squawking well above the shore
Or the roaring of the ocean
As it *crashes* against the rocks

I would like to paint
The twinkling stars
That dot and dash
across the sky
as the world spins
round day by day

I should like to paint
my fearfulness as I
Jump off the top board
And land in the pool with a
Gi-normous
Splash

Hannah L Davies (11) Earls Hall Junior School

WATER

A place of birth.
Life to fish.
A place of history.
Silky waters.
The mysteries of water.
Source of life.
A home to creatures.
A shark's lair.
A place of death.
A place of life.
Silvery waters.
A home to whales.

Emily Winckless (10) Earls Hall Junior School

WATER

A rushing waterfall
Homes for many sea creatures.
To quench your thirst
for people to have days out
for sports like
Swimming
Surfing
Water skiing
for fishing.
A sea of your thoughts
Silvery liquid
A place of all your adventures.

Hayley Jarvis (9) Earls Hall Junior School

RAINFORESTS

I would like to paint the silence in the trees,
I would like to paint the eeeeeerie look in a tiger's eye,
I would like to paint the falling of the leaves
Gently swooping from the sky,
I would like to paint the silvery glitter as a frog
Hops behind a leaf,
I would like to paint the worm that slithers underneath,
I would like to paint the startled look in a creature's eye
As the tiger pounces goodbye rabbit goodbye!

Sonia Nisbet (10) Earls Hall Junior School

DREAMS

In the dark of night when I'm in my bed, whilst I'm asleep,
thoughts come into my head.

I dream that I'm at Wembley, Captain of my team, I score the
winning goal, And all the crowd scream!

I dream I've won an Olympic medal in the 100 metres sprint
The next day in the newspaper I see my name in print!

I dream that I'm a golfer somewhere in the sun, I play
the best that I can do and score a hole in one!

I dream that I'm a snooker champion in the final once again,
I score a magnificent 147 and the crowd all chant my name!

I dream I'm racing at Silverstone going over 100 miles per hour,
Damon Hill comes round the bend but I beat him with my power!

I must stop all this dreaming, wake up, it's time for school,
I wonder what I'll dream tonight, going to bed is really cool!

Daniel Kenton (11) Earls Hall Junior School

POLLUTION

Pollution, pollution
Is anyone out there?
Look Look
Please stare
Smoke Smoke
Appearing out everywhere
Trees Trees
Being burnt
Ducks and pond life
Coated with oil
Rubbish Rubbish
Look out there
Gas Gas
Unleashed everywhere
Planes Planes
Polluting the air
Boats Boats
From quay to quay
Oil slicks trailing behind
Sewers Sewers
Leaking out into rivers
Turning the water greasy
Have you got the message
Into your skulls
You have to start
Doing Something!

David Spencer (10) Earls Hall Junior School

I'D LIKE TO PAINT

I should like to paint the sound
of a jet engine revving up.

I'd like to paint the heat as you
get off the holiday plane.

I'd like to paint the noise of the
waves crashing against the sand
on a hot summer's night.

And the sound of lightning as it
cracks into the clouds.

I'd like to paint the sound of
raindrops dripping in a puddle.

I'd like to hear the glistening of
the snowflakes that fall in
winter.

And I'd like to paint the crunch
of the snow as I walk.

I'd like to hear and paint the
sound of freedom.

Emma Derbridge (11) Earls Hall Junior School

THE MIGHTY GOD

Powerful as soldiers
Large and mighty
As dark as smoke
Killing people
Lots of noises
Knives sharpened to the top
Angry and fierce
Crashing and fighting
Spilt blood everywhere
Scared people running away
Explosions!
A ferocious God
Like thunder
Crash!

Ayesha Zaher (9) Earls Hall Junior School

POEM

A yellow and orange top
a blue bottom
a hot wavy flame,
red wax,
then Miss Kane put a match
in the white vapour then
it lit it was fun.
And we made some notes
drew the yellow and orange
and blue flames, red wax
and white vapour.

Naomi Gooch (10) Earls Hall Junior School

I WOULD LIKE TO PAINT

I would like to listen and paint the sound
Of ants scurrying across the mud.

I would like to paint the sound of orang-utans
Jumping through the trees.

I would like to paint the sound of animals just
Being born.

I would like to paint the speed of motorbikes passing by.

I would like to paint my mum and dad feeding my
Baby brother.

Katy Roper (10) Earls Hall Junior School

A MOONLIT GARDEN

In a garden lit by moonlight,
I stood admiring the beauty of nature.
The owls swooped from their trees,
the dew on the grass sparkled,
and the trees whispered secretly
to themselves every time they moved.
As I was just about to walk inside,
I decided I would come out every night,
just to look,
at a garden as beautiful,
as the moon itself.

Rachel Louise Charman (8) Earls Hall Junior School

MARS THE GOD OF WAR

Help!

The great glowing powerful God of War,
Sharp magic pointy blades,
Digging painfully
Into bloody flesh,
Oh, beware of Mars the great God of War,
Do not enter his dingy domain,
For you might end up as afternoon lunch
For the God of War.

Francesca Chambers (8) Earls Hall Junior School

SUMMER

Summer time lots of fun
Children playing in the sun.
The buzzing of bees,
the warm summer breeze
and flowers covering the ground.
The air is fresh,
the grass is green
Summer is my favourite scene.
Rounders, cricket, bat and ball
Summer's the best season of them all.

Alexandra Moyes (11) Earls Hall Junior School

SUNRISE

The sun is rising over a hill
Birds are singing loud and shrill
The world is waking
The sun is baking.

Morning is here once more,
A busy day lays in store,
The sheep 'baa' the cows 'moo'
Morning is here clear and true.

Lauren McLeod (11) Earls Hall Junior School

PROTECT

Protect
rain forests,
oceans,
trees,
endangered animals.
We care but you don't.
Trees cut all the time.

You hate the
environment!

Every one except you likes
nature.
Vandalism
in
rainforests full
of trees.
Nature is killed
most people like the
environment but you don't
care about nature
trees and animals

Steven Crick (9) Earls Hall Junior School

ONCE UPON A SPACE

I am the spaceman up in space
Up in the sky a beautiful place
I can see the stars shining bright
Pouring out buckets of light.

Up with the stars at a tremendous height
Looking down at a wonderful sight
Floating on and on never stopping, Why?
Up with the stars way up high.

The movement so slow, not fast
Very still, motionless, vast
Floating slowly far away
No time to talk or play.

The moon shimmering, silvery white
A shining, glistening, glowing sight,
Is it a balloon, a banana or a ball?
Is it white plate on a starry wall?

A golden yellow shining carriage
Or a daffodil losing its petals
Maybe fiery golden drop
Or just a spiral of golden metals.

Cecillia Makonyola (11) Earls Hall Junior School

SUMMER AUTUMN WINTER SPRING

Summer is the right time of year,
When children and adults have water fights,
And clap their hands and cheer,
And autumn is when people fly kites,
And get the angles right,
Winter, you get out the wine,
Because it's Christmas time,
Spring, you should watch the plants get higher,
While watching the snow get lower.

Jennifer Martinali (11) Earls Hall Junior School

YOU'RE

Happy as a fluffy white cloud,
Excited like a jumping bean.
As tall as a tower,
As clever as a computer,
Hardworking like a farmer.
As wise as a right decision,
As gentle as a feather falling on your hand:
You paint a world of wonder.

Hollie Bernardo (9) Epping Upland CE Primary School

RED

A child lies in bed, then the fighting begins . . .
Angry remarks thrown through the air,
Huge, painful dents in the child's heart.
'Why, oh why, won't they stop?'
The child wonders.
Each night the child dreads,
For each night the fighting continues.
Smash! Crash!
Objects gliding through the air,
Missing heads and arms by inches,
Then quiet.
The child thinks they've stopped,
But again the fighting begins.
How much longer will this continue?
Half an hour later all is quiet.
Most children's nights are filled by black.
This child's are filled with worry
Dead and red . . .

Kimberley Freeman (11) Epping Upland CE Primary School

YOU'RE

You're as happy as bees dancing around
On a hot summer's day.
You're a warm feeling
Like the sun beaming down on me.
You're as funny
As a one-person comedy show.
You're as dangerous as a lion
Gnawing at an antelope.
You're as distracting
As a fly buzzing around my head.

Sarah Skinner (8) Epping Upland CE Primary School

CHRISTMAS MORNING

Christmas morning
Is like a massive freezer
Has been in your garden
And trees have been frozen.

Andrew Hanson (8) Epping Upland CE Primary School

MY PETS

I have loads of pets
And I play with them all day,
But my cat jumped over the wall
And my mouse has got away.
My rabbit is on the sofa
My lizard is on the run,
The dog won't stop barking
And the camel spat at my mum.
My pig is rolling in the mud
My llama is a pain,
I caught another mouse
The gorilla likes the rain.
Now I have a bumble bee
I'm just telling you now,
I get on just fine
With my new pet cow.

Sarah Gunning (10) Fairhouse Junior School

DOGS

Bertie Mo and little James
All like playing puppy games
Spot, Dotty and Fifi too
Will be happy playing ball with you
But *old* Dusty won't want to play
He's happy to lay asleep all day.

Louise Peck (8) Fairhouse Junior School

A HOMELESS OLD WOMAN

What do I see? People,
What are they thinking as they look at me?
A homeless old woman,
Without any home,
Walking the streets all on my own,
With a tatty old bag,
And tatty old shoes,
Starving and thirsty,
And I haven't any food,
So what do I see,
What am I thinking,
When you've got a home,
Walking the streets,
All on my own.

Rosanne Davison (11) Fairhouse Junior School

LIVING WITH A MONSTER

Living with a monster
Is like living with a sister
Like getting fed to a frog
And green soup, it's horrible
There's all lumps of eyeballs, toes
And fingers. Living with a monster is horrible
But it's better than eating mum's roast dinner
With horrible peppers and onions like
Silly red Caterpillars.
It's better living with a monster
With bulgy skin, sharp claws, he even gives
Me nightmares, very scary ones in a big
Bed of snakes and spiders.

Callum Finn (10) Fairhouse Junior School

THE WIND

The wind was blowing to and fro among
the trees.
Blowing and picking up waters from
the seas.
Blowing in the darkness back and forth
and whistling softly on its way.
Blowing people's hats away
Enjoys itself,
Before the wind goes away.

Peu Lamm Cheung (10) Gascoigne Junior School

THE WIND

The wind is in the air
The wind is here and there.
It comes at you while you walk.
It stabs you hard like a fork.
The wind is hard and knocks you over
Sometimes it whistles and gets harder and harder.
It comes hard and then dies down.
Waiting for the next time you'll be around.

Abby Gibson (10) Gascoigne Junior School

SOMEONE'S COMING UP THE STAIRS

Someone's coming up the stairs,
It could be a dragon or a monster or some bears.

Someone's coming up the stairs
It could have ugly skin, or hairs.

Oh what shall I do,
Oh what shall I do,
I don't know who,
I don't know who.

It's coming towards the door of fog
Here it is
Here it is
Oh it's my dog!

Sally Thwaites (9) Grafton Junior School

MY RABBIT SHANDY

My rabbit lives in a hutch
She loves to be cuddled and touched,
She is fluffy and sandy,
So I named her Shandy.
I let her out in the sun
for a little run.
My little bunny, she is so funny.
My rabbit in the garden she hops
about and plays. She has big and fluffy floppy
ears.
Her favourite food is carrots.
I'm glad I have a rabbit and not a parrot.

Danielle Leaver (9) Grafton Junior School

VIKING SETTLEMENT

Vikings are brave
Vikings are strong
Some are tall
Some are small
Round and round
They sail ships
Ready for battle
Against them all

Adrian Brown (9) Grafton Junior School

VIKINGS ARE BRAVE

Vikings are brave
Vikings are mean
And tough from
Norway and Denmark
The Vikings set
Forth to raid
And kill
For these Vikings
Are nothing but
Trouble.

Christopher Conway (9) Grafton Junior School

SECRETS

I've got to keep a secret,
I'm not allowed to tell,
If I tell my friend,
She will really yell,
I can't tell my teacher,
I can't tell my mum,
And if I tell my dad,
He'll be really glum,
It's nothing really scary,
It's nothing really bad,
It's only I've got a boyfriend,
And he's a really cute lad!

Natalie Smith (11) Grafton Junior School

FOOD FOR THOUGHT

I was sitting at home one boring day,
When all of the food suddenly started to play,
A lump of big brown juicy beef,
Was dancing with a lettuce leaf.
A little orange tangerine,
Was kissing a big green runner-bean.
Some carrots and some plain white rice,
Were skipping with some smelly spice.
A piece of lovely sticky toffee,
Was diving into a cuppa coffee,
Then a giant blob of cream,
Came flying towards me . . . Phew it was just a dream!

Danielle Caton (11) Grafton Junior School

THE DEADLY SHARK

The shark swims around you
And he sees you.
Once he has seen you he'll lay
As still as he can and wait.
Once you get in his sight,
He'll give you a nasty bite.
He won't give you a warning
Not even in the morning.
He'll grab your leg and pull you down
And under water you will drown.

Brian Martin (11) Grafton Junior School

THE WHALE SHARK

Broad and blunt is the whale shark's head.
He sleeps on seaweed for his bed
He breathes in sandy waters
And then goes out and slaughters
All the little animals he kills
I wonder if he eats electric eels?

Natalie Garrett (11) Grafton Junior School

THE MONSTER

My monster lives under my bed,
Or sometimes it lives in the shed.
Norman is the monster's name,
Shame he's not very tame.
Time to time he makes a noise,
Ever so often he breaks my toys.
Really he is quite a friend,
Someday, I know, this will end.

Lisa Davie (11) Grafton Junior School

MY SISTER

My terrible sister
Is like a big blister.
She picks up sticky worms.
Then she gets horrible germs.
She loves to eat chewy sweets,
She makes my mum get her treats.
She doesn't have to eat her greens,
And all she eats is sausages and
beans!

Danielle Webb (10) Grafton Junior School

FOOD

I came home from school one day
When all the food had started to play.
The fish laid on the dish
A blob of custard danced with mustard.
A buttered bun was having fun,
There were tangerines and runner-beans.
A fat big fork kissed a leg of pork,
A lump of toffee drank some coffee.
Suddenly it all came to a stop!
The rice crispies didn't pop.
The buttered bun stopped having fun
The custard stopped dancing with mustard
There wasn't any tangerines or runner-beans
The fat big fork kissed the leg of pork
The lump of toffee spilt the coffee
And everything was back to normal again.

Michelle Barry (10) Grafton Junior School

SHARKS

Sharks eat human flesh
They never are tidy they make a mess,
Blood and guts everywhere,
Sharks just do not care,
They're never satisfied,
With one human two humans three or four,
They always want much, much more,
Their teeth are big and very sharp,
People kill them with something called a
harp,
But when people try to kill them
back,
They always try to attack.

Lauren Brown (11) Grafton Junior School

DINOSAURS

There it stood right in
front of us.
With its great huge jaws
And enormous eyes
Looking down at us.
We start to run
And so did it
It caught
Us up.
Oh, no!
It's too late,
We're the beast's dinner!

Stewart Gamage (11) Grafton Junior School

SWIMMING

I like to go swimming twice a week.
To train and enter galas and reach my peak.
Back-stroke breast-stroke I do them all.
But most of all I love front-crawl.
I splash around and kick my legs.
Keep going faster my coach begs,
I reach the end of my race,
And I know I have come first place.

Craig Sullivan (9) Grafton Junior School

NETBALL

Netball is brill
It's a really good game
It may look like basketball
But it isn't the same

You've got to be fit
To play in this sport
To beat the other team
When you're on court

Players you mark
Don't let you get the ball
You've got to ignore this
And don't fall

When we play
Winning is our aim
So come and cheer us
Through the wind and rain

Sarah Chance (9) Grafton Junior School

DUCKS

Waddling round our school garden,
Went the mother duck and her new babies,
They waddle here they waddle there,
Then we come to feed them,
They eat and eat and they still want more,
Then they go for a swim in the pond,
They splash around just like us at a swimming pool,
Then it's time for them to sleep,
And time for us to retreat!

Lee Cable (9) Grafton Junior School

THE DAY OF THE TELEVISION

You turn the switch, sit back and relax,
You watch the screen and wait for the programme you want,
Bursting with news, reviews and previews,
It's very exciting to see the News at Ten.
To see the speakers vibrate with volume,
To also see the vibrant colours,
I like documentaries and TV tunes,
I use my remote to turn to BBC1
Then I change channels to Sky TV
You see news, cartoons, discoveries and sports
My dad prefers the football and the cricket,
While I like cartoons and the news,
Very soon David Frost's on the telly,
Then Wildlife on One.
What a good job my TV had done.

Marc Grayston (10) Grafton Junior School

THE SCREAM

A scream echoed through the night,
It made my hair turn white,
It bounced off walls,
And made ripples in swimming pools,
I was scared and frightened,
My skin seemed to tighten,
I turned on my light,
I was alright,
There were ripples in *my* dream,
I heard a scream,
I turned off my light,
A scream echoed through the night.

Samantha Chase (10) Grove Junior School

THE SCREAM

A scream echoed through the night
It was someone screaming
I was terrified I thought it was a German
Then I heard it again I was really frightened now
I heard glass shattering
Then I heard people moving but there was nobody there but me
I heard a bomb go off and I saw smoke coming from the place
Where the scream was
A scream echoed through the night.

Eleanor Clarke (9) Grove Junior School

ME AND THE SNAIL

I look down at the little snail,
Still tucked down in his house.
Sitting there he's motionless,
Not a problem in his life.
I would like to be a snail,
Camouflaged in the grass.
He slithers along slowly
As he stretches out his eyes.
If I was a little snail
I would have a house to myself.
Humans have to work all day,
But snails have a lovely life.

How can he be jealous
Of an ugly snail like me
Going along slowly,
And sticking onto things?
I would like to be a human,
Walking running playing.
Having fun on the grass
Or anywhere they please.
I have to carry my house,
Which is lumped up on my back.
We can't jump while sticking on things,
Humans have a lovely life!

Sara Lewis (10) Grove Junior School

SILVER

The snow queen of fairy tales
Glistens in the snow,
A misty diamond crystal
Is on her icy hand,
Lakes of cold frosted ice,
Sparkling glitter.

Lucy Hockey (11) Grove Junior School

MY DAD

My dad is very clever,
he knows all kinds of things,
When I have a question,
I always ask for him.

Dad - how do cars go?
Dad - why is the sky blue?
Dad - who makes it snow?
Dad - will I get as big as you?

He always knows the answers,
and he's never ever wrong.
Sometimes it annoys me,
because his answers are so long.

But mostly when I ask him,
Dad - do you want a game of snooker?
Dad - do you want to play football?
Dad - can you fix my computer?
My dad can do it all.

Anthony Risidore (10) Grove Junior School

THE DRIPPING TAPS

The two bath taps are dripping,
Splish, splash, splosh,
Alternately,
One by one,
Splish, splash, splosh,
The drips slide down the plughole,
Where they stop,
Nobody knows,
But for now,
All I hear is,
Splish, splash, splosh.

Katherine Lattaway (11) Grove Junior School

THE DRIP

Drip,
A drop of water falls down from the tap,
The drop is crystal clear,
It hits the peach sink,
And runs around the plug hole,
Like it's in a race,
Plop, drip,
It falls down the plug hole,
As another drip appears from the tap,
Ready to be as pretty as the first.

Sarah Wotherspoon (11) Grove Junior School

FIREWORKS

Whiz whoosh go the fireworks.
Lots of children lots of laughter.
Zoom goes the Roman candle
Whiz bang here comes the fountain
Swirls down then the laughter
And fire dies down.
All that's left of
Guy Fawkes
Are ashes and shreds of clothes.

Ashley Perkins (8) Grove Junior School

ZOOMING FIREWORKS

November the 5th is a special night,
With fireworks and bonfires too.
Whiz goes the Catherine Wheel,
Whoosh goes the Rocket.
And a shower of rain from the
Fountain.
All the fireworks dazzle,
And you have bonfire food too.
You have hot potatoes
And hot dogs too.
The bonfire crackles and flicks
It also has lots of flames,
Sometimes you have Guys,
And sometimes you have none.

Kate Alderton (9) Grove Junior School

THE OWL

One silent night there was an owl.
It was a very starry night.
The owl lived on the very top branch
of the oak tree.
It was listening very carefully for its prey.
That night there was bright moonlight.
He heard rustling in the leaves.
There was no wind that night.
It was all calm.
He could hear very well.
He hovered above his prey.
To make sure there were no foxes
Lurking in the bushes.
Then he glided silently to his prey
He grabbed the little animal.
He was a hungry owl.
He gobbled his prey.
That was the end of him.

Lucy Bowhay (8) Grove Junior School

RAIN

Wet dripping water,
Running down your neck,
Like little diamonds dropping.
Rain falling from the sky,
Sharp and fast.
Splashing puddles,
Drizzle everywhere.

Helen Harris (11) Grove Junior School

THE SEA

The sea is like a pack of
white horses,
Tossing their manes,
As they gallop towards the
shore,
They rear up,
And their hooves kick up
froth,
When the sun comes out,
They retreat,
Lay down,
Calm,
And occasionally flick their
tails.

Charlotte Ford (11) Grove Junior School

GREEN

A peaceful meadow
With wildlife and trees,
Singing birds
The roar of the sea,
A cottage in the distance
A farm on the hill,
The scent of flowers
So perfect and still,
The warmth of July
The freshness of dew,
The animals prancing
And the trees blowing too.

Marie Turner (11) Grove Junior School

THE SEA

Sometimes grey and sometimes blue,
Sometimes has a misty hue,
Sometimes rough and sometimes mild,
Sometimes smooth and sometimes wild.
It spreads around for all to see.
What is this thing? It is the sea.

Adam Williams (11) Grove Junior School

WATERFALL

Water crashing down
On the crystal clear water below,
Tumbling down like a giant avalanche.
Diamonds sprinkle over the rocks,
Causing a fine mist
Resplendent in the mid-day sun.
The sun scintillates off the water
Beaming brightly,
Reflecting the clear blue sky.
A twinkle in the eyes of the people watching,
The crystal dazzling them.
The day begins to end,
The swiftness of the water
Passionately flows down stream.
Night falls,
The water calms, to an end.

Graeme Roberts (10) Grove Junior School

WATER

You can hear the crashing against the rocks.
Tumbling down like rapids.
The water is rough,
And it slashes as it rushes swiftly along.
When you touch it,
It is cold.
It is as cold as ice and very chilly.
You'll see that it is clear,
But reflecting the sky.

Charlene Hoy (11) Grove Junior School

MY TREE

I planted a tree in September
It grew until December
Then it suddenly stopped
When it got to the top
And really that's all I remember.

Kerry O'Brine (11) Highwoods Primary School

SPIDERS SNAP

Spiders in the living room
Spiders on the stairs
A spider could be anywhere
So you better beware.

A spider behind the door
Or even on the floor
It could be on the wall
But! Watch out it might fall.

Nikki Kemzura (9) Holly Trees County Junior School

LEAVES

Leaves leaves,
in the trees.

Leaves leaves,
up in the sky.

Leaves leaves,
red, green, brown and yellow.

Leaves leaves,
fresh trees.

Leaves leaves,
flying bees.

Catherine Woodman (10) Holly Trees County Junior School

LADYBIRD

Ladybird, ladybird
round and
small
dotted black
and sitting by
the pool

Spider spider
on the
chair
watch out
it might
be on
the stair.

Ashley Pretlove (10) Holly Trees County Junior School

BUILDING

Once I built a sandcastle
The biggest in the land
I made it out of sand
I bet it was the biggest
I've never seen one before
Then I saw another one
No it can't be phew, what a relief

Ceri Roberts (8) Holly Trees County Junior School

TEDDY

T eddies are what you cuddle at night.

E asy to fall asleep with.

D reaming about your teddy,

D reaming the happiest thoughts,

Y ou do love your teddy as much
as this poem don't you?

Natalie May Osburn (9) Holt Farm County Junior School

THE SCHOOL HOLIDAYS

When the school holidays come,
having lots of fun,
no work to be done,
no more teacher looks and boring books,
no more tears and no more sorrow,
Because we don't need to go to school tomorrow!

Judy Law (11) Holt Farm County Junior School

THE SEA SHORE

Wind rushing through my hair,
waves dashing against the rocks,
foam bubbling dirty, murky,
seagulls calling while the rain
is falling.

Lots of people laughing and cheering,
running round and playing ball and
some resting on the sand.

Laura E Deaves (11) Holt Farm County Junior School

SUMMER BREEZE

The waves lapped the shore,
Squawking seagulls,
Soaring high,
Roaring sea,
Silky sand,
Slipping between my toes.
A soft summer breeze,
Drifting through my hair.

A baby blue sky,
Glittering golden sun,
Misty horizon,
Sparkling sea,
Shimmering at sunset,
Silence, calm, hushed, stopped.
A soft summer breeze,
Drifting through my hair.

Kellie Louise Osburn (11) Holt Farm County Junior School

FRIENDSHIP

Friends are there when you need them
Reliable friends will pass the test
Impressive friends are the best
Either way they are great
Nevertheless whatever way it goes they are faithful
Doubt is a way of testing friendship
Sadly not all friendships last

Lindsey Hayward (11) Holt Farm County Junior School

AIR RAID SHELTER

Bang crash goes the
bombs and the planes.

Run run hide in the shelter
before we get bombed and
we will all die.

Take your food and your
drinks, covers and games to
keep you warm, cold and hungry
under the ground I want to
go home into my own bed
and to sleep peacefully again.

Jenny Dent (11) John Bunyan Junior School

A WAR POEM

The big planes swoop, shooting and bombing,
The lights go out, it's very dim,
We run to a shelter it's cold inside,
Sick babies crying,
Hurt people dying
The sun is rising the darkness fades,
But tomorrow is the same as today.

Danny Hankin (11) John Bunyan Junior School

WORLD WAR 2

Carrying my mask,
Is quite a task.
My shoulder is sore,
With this strap I wore.
I walk to the shop with it,
I want to kick it.
Bombs fall down,
It makes me frown.
Dead bodies lying around,
Not making a sound.
Of course they're dead,
They're bombed to a shred.
Then there are screams,
As I watch blood go by in streams.
My mum drags me to the shed, or I shall be dead.
Soon there shall be peace and all shall be free!
These were my thoughts in 1943.

Vicky Sayward (11) John Bunyan Junior School

DOG FIGHT

Planes flying in the air,
Bang, bang, dog fight, dog fight,
The siren wails as Germans fly over,
Smash, Britons killed,
One less soldier to feed,
One more family ruined.

Back up in the air,
Bang, bang, dog fight, dog fight,
Smash, German killed,
One less battle to fight,
One more German to bury.

Liam Baker (11) John Bunyan Junior School

DOG FIGHT

In the air a dogfight starts
With guns and bombs in hand.

Guns blazing everywhere
Bullets flying through the air.

German planes and English planes
Going close and shooting guns.

One gets shot down
The other survives.

One gets to fly away
And shoot its guns another day.

Michael Leipper (11) John Bunyan Junior School

GERMANS!

They shaved our long hair off
They snatched, they killed
Germans!
They told us we were having a shower
But we weren't
Germans!
We were cold and wet
Then we heard a sound
Germans!
Some began to cough
Some were falling
Germans!
We screamed
Some were dying
Germans!

Natalie Crysell (11) John Bunyan Junior School

RATION BOOKS

Everything nowadays is rations
From sweets to veg and fruit.
I look in the shops at the empty cookie jars
Oh why does everything have to be rations?

I have to save up if I want a new coat
Or a new dress or even a nice new pair of shoes,
A hat or a scarf
Oh why does everything have to be rations?

Katy Mott (11) John Bunyan Junior School

MY SHADOW

My shadow under the sun walking along beside
Me.
Always with me wherever I go.
Always hangs around with me always been my
Friend. When I speak to it it doesn't answer
But I understand my shadow is my friend
Forever.

Lianne Roberts (8) Kingston CP School

MY SHADOW

When I sunbathe my shadow sunbathes
with me. My shadow comes to school with
me, he sits in the classroom with me
he never talks he never eats but loves
to run up and down with me and he
never gets told off. My shadow comes
home with me he has tea with me
and then we both go to bed.

Victor McNeely (7) Kingston CP School

THE BERLIN WALL

There was a young boy called
Paul.
Who jumped in a swimming pool.
And he passed a friend
Who was round the bend
Then Paul saw the Berlin Wall.

Shaun Lock (9) Lawford C of E School

THE MAN WHO EATS A POISONOUS PIE

There was a person from Leeds
Who started to dig up his weeds
He didn't know why
He'd ate a poisonous pie
And he turned into a big fat seed.

He didn't know why he was a seed,
So he couldn't sit down to feed,
So he sat on his seat
And ate his shredded wheat
Then he turned into a bead.

Chloe Read (8) Lawford C of E School

THE PIG

There was a young pig
Who was wearing a wig
And he picked up a twig
So he went in the barn
And he did no harm
Then he started to dig

Adam Smith (9) Lawford C of E School

THE ONION

There was a young man from
      London,
Who grew a massive onion,
Then he cried and cried
Until he fried
The great big massive onion.

Mark Mills (9) Lawford C of E School

SUN

The sun is bright
The sun is beautiful
When it is out
It is lovely and
It is lovely when
We go swimming in the sun.

Douglas Fryer (9) Lawford C of E School

ALL ABOUT PAM

There was a young girl called Pam
She used to live opposite a dam
The dam flooded twice
Then she found two big mice
And she gave them to a boy called Sam

Victoria Brooks (9) Lawford C of E School

THE YOUNG PEOPLE WHO DRANK FROM A TUB

There was a young man from Lawford
Who saw a young man from Flatford
They went to a pub
They drank from the tub
Then went home with Cindy Crawford

Hannah Pratt (9) Lawford C of E School

DAPPLED

I put my horse up for hire
A lady came to try him
She whipped him, she beat him
She rode him through the mire
I'll never let my horse now,
For any lady's hire

Danielle Springett (10) Lawford C of E School

WINTER

Winter cold
weather not
quite so hot.

                Weather cold
                snows a lot
                sleeping baby in her cot.

Winter cold
weather not
quite so hot.

                Weather cold
                snows a lot
                waking baby in her cot.

Winter cold
weather not
quite so hot.

                Break of morn
                cock-crow of dawn.
                White snow across our front lawn.

Louise Appleby (8) Lawford C of E School

THE LION AND THE MEERKAT

There was once a lion called Peter
Who met a meerkat called Rita
He bumped into her and said oh dear me
Would you like to come for tea?
Then she said no thanks mate
Or I'll be late
For my nice hot bath you see

Daniel Chamberlain (9) Lawford C of E School

DIVORCE

Henry the 8th, the cruel and mean, decided to
divorce.
'Oh no my love' cried sad old Anne until
her voice was hoarse.
But Henry, with his mind made up,
told her just to go.
To some far off place like Braintree
or Harlow.
So Anne left reluctantly what else could
she do?
And that I tell you is most definitely true!

Jonathan Taylor (10) Lawford C of E School

WHEN I GROW UP

When I grow up I want to be a lorry driver,
driving down the road
at 60 miles per hour,
then at the end of the journey we'd
unload.

When I grow up I want to be a footballer,
to run up the pitch and score a goal,
to be Man of the Match in every game
just like Andy Cole.

When I grow up I want to be a sailor,
bobbing up and down on the waves,
to go fishing and catch a fish,
and to go exploring in the caves.

Mark Thurlow (10) Lawford C of E School

MY SECRET PENPAL

On the weekends I used to sit,
All day long in my little sandpit.
Till one bright morning I had
an idea,
To write to my friend who
lived near Clacton pier.
I kept the letters in a drawer,
And didn't let anyone know.
Until one night my friend
found out,
And she chucked them in
the bin.

Piia Jeffries (9) Lawford C of E School

THOUGHTS

Good thoughts,
Bad thoughts,
Happy thoughts,
Sad thoughts,
All kinds of thoughts.
Whizz round in your head,
Like when is bed?
What's the answer to all these thoughts?
Just some time to think.
Like how many times a day do you blink?
When's the next lesson?
When's the next play?
All these thoughts take a lot of thinking,
So think fast, think quick or they'll be gone in
                                      a blinking.

Claire Appleby (10) Lawford C of E School

HENRY'S WIVES

Divorced, beheaded, died, divorced, beheaded, survived
First came Catherine of Aragon, she was divorced,
Just forgotten like a horse
Divorced, beheaded, died, divorced, beheaded, survived
Then there was Anne Boleyn, she was beheaded
                              the thing she most dreaded
Divorced, beheaded, died, divorced, beheaded, survived
Then Jane Seymour, she just died
Divorced, beheaded, died, divorced, beheaded, survived
Anne of Cleaves came next and she was divorced.
Divorced, beheaded, died, divorced, beheaded, survived
Then came Catherine Howard, she was beheaded
                              not shredded
Divorced, beheaded, died, divorced, beheaded, survived
And last of all Catherine Parr, she out lived Henry by far.

Alexea Williams (10) Lawford C of E School

A SARDINE RACE

There was once a sardine
Swimming in a race with a lovely face.
He was winning, he was swimming very
Fast. Then he was coming last.
Soon he caught up, then he had a rest,
And put on a bright yellow vest.
Then he saw the finishing tape
And came second behind his mate.

Mark Kemp (10) Lawford C of E School

CATS ON THE LOOSE

Cats are raiding rubbish bins,
Clattering lids, oh what a din!
In the night, lights go on,
Windows open and people shout:
'We are trying to sleep.'

Elizabeth Percival (9) Lawford C of E School

MY DOG KIZZIE

My dog Kizzie's completely mad,
She runs round the garden at 100 miles an hour
She annoys my mum and trips up my dad.
And when we shout at her she whines and cowers,
And she tears the petals off our flowers.

She thinks she's a human,
She sits in our armchairs.
To get food she always has a crafty plan.
And she likes chasing rabbits and hares.

Once she took a five pound note,
We try to stop her being naughty but we always fail.
She chewed up my best toy boat,
And she chases her tail.

She is very naughty but when I am sad
She licks me,
So she's not that bad!

Sarah McLachlan (9) Lawford C of E School

EMERGENCY

Ne-nor there goes a police car
With its lights flashing blue
I wonder what happened
What did someone do
There goes a fire engine
With its lights flashing blue
Is there a fire
Is it true

There goes an ambulance
With its lights flashing blue
Is someone hurt?
I don't know
I'm going to see
What has happened
Oh-no it's our house
Mum, Dad, are you OK.
Did you know what happened
Or did Dad try to fix the cooker!

Mark Munt (10) Lawford C of E School

ANIMALS ANIMALS

Cats have fur,
Dogs have tails,
Ladybirds have spots
Like chicken pox.

Birds have wings,
Fishes have fins,
At night you just might
See a badger in the bins.

Maria Leonard (10) Lawford C of E School

DRAWING

I like drawing
It's something to do
I like drawing people
And funny ones too.

I like drawing animals
Falling fast asleep
I like drawing them
When they're playing hide and seek.

Zoë Clark (10) Lawford C of E School

ARSENAL

Arsenal, Arsenal are the best,
'Cause they always beat the rest.
With Bergkamp, Merson, Seaman and Wright
For the championship there is no fight.

Schwarz in midfield, Merson too,
Bergkamp and Wright will score a few.
Seaman in goal best in the league,
Adams best captain by far in the lead.

Highbury's the ground,
In the 1800s it was found.
Arsenal is in north London,
Rivals with teams like Tottenham.

David Wright (10) Lawford C of E School

SPRING

Spring is sunny
spring is bright
Chicks are hatching in the spring
light
Mums are bathing
children are playing
And in a nearby field horses
are neighing
And the dads are at work
eating a bun
While the rest of us are
just having fun.

Sarah Parker (10) Lawford C of E School

THE PLAYGROUND

Children playing
Children running
Children screaming
Children eating
Children drinking
Children sitting
Children walking
Teachers watching
Teachers standing
Looking all around
Children hopping
Children jumping like a kangaroo
Children playing it
Children playing Bulldog
Children having great fun . . .
In the playground.

Emma Page (8) Lawford C of E School

RUGBY CRAZY

The beaten finalists in 1991 believe they can go
one better this time. With the likes of Carling,
Andrew, and the Underwood brothers.
I wonder will they do it?

They'll meet the likes of Australia, South Africa and
New Zealand who will rely on the ability of Jonah Loma
I wonder will they do it?

Rob Andrew - now England's record points scorer of all
time - continues to flourish at fly half and there's
Captain Will Carling.
I wonder will they do it?

Jeremy Guscot is back to full fitness in the
centre. The new names of Catt, Bracken, Rodber
and Ubogu will all be a key part to England's
success.
I wonder will they do it?

Robert Abbott (10) Lawford C of E School

SPORTS' DAY

I did sports' day
I won a sack race
But at the scores
Yellow team won
My team came second
But all at once
I hear a noise
It was yellow team
They had won the cup
They cheered
'Hurrah we won.'

Rhian Barrick (8) Lawford C of E School

PLAYGROUND POEM

It's summer it's summer
It's nice and warm
Children playing on the lawn

Boys play football
Girls play netball
Other girls watch

Sometimes you are
Allowed on the grass

Follow the path
What do you
See a weeping branch
Sit under the tree.

When you go down
One of the paths
You are at the shed
There are little trees.

You can see flower beds
With nice plants and there
Are some picnic benches
People sit on them, and eat at break on them

Kayleigh Toner (8) Lawford C of E School

GHOSTS AND GHOULS

The story of ghosts and ghouls.
Ghosts in the house,
Ghouls in the garden,
They come out at night,
And give you a fright,
And they die when they see the light.

You see them they die,
You hurt them they cry,
I am scared of ghosts,
I am scared of ghouls
But at least it's the end of *both*.

Louie Nutt (8) Lawford C of E School

SPORTS' DAY

Blue
Sports' day is today
I like sports' day
I'm in the blue team
My best friend is in the yellow
Teacher blows the whistle,
Off the track we go
Running running down the track.
We go zooming down the track
As fast as we can go.

Red
My mum and dad are watching
I'm really going fast
Clare's dad's filming us
Running, running, running.

Yellow

The winning team are the yellows
Then the reds,
But last of all
Blue team with fifty nine points.

Laura Louise Gentry (8) Lawford C of E School

POLLUTION

P oisoned rivers
O il spills in the sea
L itter all around
L ook what's happening to our world
U ntidy streets
T idy up, don't drop litter
I gnorant people should know better
O ur world is getting polluted with rubbish
N ow it's up to us.

Adam Monahan

MAY BLOSSOM

Clouds of strawberry tinged blossom
Smother the hawthorn tree.
Standing out against the sea blue
Sky like a powdery snow drift.
The magnolia and raspberry confetti
Drops on the chestnut brown twig.
Pearlised delicate tears cascade
From the slender branch, forming
A carpet of snow on the grass below.
The obsidian and ochre bees buzz
Around carrying the golden pollen
From anther to stigma.

Katie Louise Cooper (11) Lincewood Junior School

CHRISTMAS

Christmas is a time of year,
with happiness
and a merry cheer.
With joyful children all around,
and pure white snow upon the ground,
and one little baby boy was born
in a stable in a cradle.

Rebekah Brewster (10) Lincewood Junior School

BLOSSOM

A soft pink cloud of blossom cascades
like fireworks on bonfire night.
It reminds me of the cold frosted snow
of winter.
As the delicate pearls sway in the breeze I
think to myself, how come the leaves are so
shiny?
Little buds grow older while protected by sepals.

Georgie Baker (11) Lincewood Junior School

HELICOPTER

H appy helicopter flying high,
E legant helicopter up in the sky.
L ovely helicopter enjoying the breeze,
I gnorant helicopter over the seas.
C hildren excited jump in the air,
O ver it flies, children stare.
P retty paint gleams in the sun,
T housands of children having fun.
E nter the helicopter, come and see,
R ound and round our special tree.

Michelle Iveson (9) Lincewood Junior School

TOWN

Birds tweet
Trains rattle
Traffic builds up.
Bins shake clutter clutter
Litter rumbles
Stones fall down drains.
Leaves crackle
Branches break.
Buildings smash
And last of all nothing there.

Luke Wyatt (9) Lincewood Junior School

WINTER HAIKU

All I see is fog
Trees metamorphosing
I'm sure I am lost

                      Drip, drip water falls
                      The heavens have now opened
                      Cloudy ashen skies

Freezing cold strong gale
Blowing trees and bushes down
Inside our brollies

                      White carpet outside
                      Icy crystals floating down
                      Icing sugared trees.

Alison Jackson (11) Lincewood Junior School

THE SEASIDE

A lonely beach where the
wind blows sand.
Water crashing against rocks.
Seagulls landing on calm water
with a soft splash.
Seaweed being pushed by
water with a swish to land.
It's like ghosts have scared
the people away.
Stones getting sucked back to
sea with a scratching scraping
sound.
Winds blowing making a
whistling whisper.

Sean Hogan (8) Lincewood Junior School

SNOW

Meandering crystalline flakes descend
haphazardly.
Gleaming ivory blanket glistening on an alabaster
ground.
Cascading fragile confetti drifts slowly on the
iced floor.
Myriads of delicate marshmallow ice crystals
glitter in the pale watery sun.
Moist crispy snow swirling gracefully.
Twisting and twirling gently.
Minute icy ballerinas dashing about energetically.
Their performance ends as they merge together on
the albescent ground.

Victoria Aley (11) Lincewood Junior School

MAY BLOSSOM

Soft pink delicate confetti cascades down like snowflakes
in clouds of blossom.
The drifting albescent and rose pink teardrops
are silhouetted against the powder blue sky.
Jasper woodland, sprinkled with magnolia candyfloss.
Chestnut twigs with smooth shiny olive leaves
sway in the woodland breeze pearlescent droplets
drift down like snow falling. Delicate perfume attracts
the dancing bees. The apple green stamens are tipped with
chocolate brown anthers. The sticky stigma collects the
lemon pollen from buzzing bees. Tiny buds hide
within the daisy tree.

Heather Ilesley (11) Lincewood Junior School

BLOSSOM

Magnolia clouds of puffy candyfloss hang on tasty
twiglet.

Raspberry tinted and milky white delicate teardrops
daintily fall to the emerald grass.

The grass is getting married. Soft pink and
gentle white confetti is drifting to the
jade ground.

Five tiny snowflakes to each tiny flower.
Thousands of these pears hang on the
chocolate brown tree.

Jennifer Clark (11) Lincewood Junior School

DAEDALUS

The day started gloomy and no hope at all.
But father and son had a plan in mind.
With one wing on each arm they set off, into the sky,
And Daedalus shouted a warning as he flew by.
Don't go too close to the water, don't go too close to the sun.
But these words were soon forgotten.
Then down
        Down
                Down
                        Went the craftsman's son.
'Help!' Icarus cried but it was too late.
No trace of his body was seen.
Just a few feathers on the surface of the sea.

Verity Sullivan (10) Lincewood Junior School

ON THE PLANE

On the plane
Next to a pain,
Here's the food,
That tastes like wood,
Writing and reading,
And of course dreaming,
9 hours straight,
Waiting and waiting,
On the plane,
Next to a pain,
Landing,
Landing,
Was it worth the waiting?

Lisa Jackson (10) Lincewood Junior School

DEAR OH DEAR!

Escape had not been easy
But they had both been brave.

Then came the doom of the poor young boy -
This was such a tragedy
When it should have been joy!
Daedalus was so very, very sad,
But then he would be -
He was the boy's dad!
He now knew the grief his wife must have felt,
He'd warned his poor boy that the wax wings would melt.
He now lives alone - no wife and no son -
What a price had been paid,
For the freedom he'd won.

Amy Copping (10) Lincewood Junior School

A FRIEND . . .

J amie is my best friend.
A friend who cares about me.
M y friend cheers me up when I'm sad.
I enjoy her company.
E verlasting friendship (hopefully).

R emembered forever,
A lmost anyway!
Y oung and full of fun.
M ighty Jamie always helping me.
O ffering advice.
N ever bossy.
D ependable and the *best!*

Grace Theobald (10) Lincewood Junior School

A DAWNING DEATH

A young girl lying in bed,
Dying,
She speaks of burial,
The family sits around the bed,
Weeping,
They speak of life before,
Happy times,
The mother pleads her not to go,
Voices can be heard through the open window,
Distant,
But happy,
The father weeps,
He is not ashamed of his grief,
The girl's sister mourns,
Crying like sand dripping from a sand timer,
The girl calls out in pain,
Surely this can't be the end,
Death fills the family's mind,
The ones left behind cry,
She breathes no more,
Her face is silent,
The chest deflates and goes limp,
Slowly, silently,
They leave the dead room,
Taking only memories of life before.

Alison Payne (11) Maldon Court School

THE ECHO

She calls,
Un-loved,
Alone,
Afraid,
All she has left is the echo,
The echo of life,
Loneliness,
Solitude,
Her life would be finished without the
Echo,
So reassuring,
Contented,
Her only friend,
When the echo dies, she dies
Her life will have gone,
Departed,
Left her,
Saying goodbye forever.

Catherine Pope (11) Maldon Court School

UNTITLED

She sits weeping,
Her wilted face unhappy.
Streaked with tired tears.
Tears of a mother who has cried for so long.
Her house,
The place she calls home, is lit by a candle.
The walls are bare.
Near her a tap drips.
Her baby, that lies in her arms is still, dead,
and lifeless.
Now all she had to live for is gone.
Her child, her home,
Gone.
She has given up.
Nothing is left for her now.
She lies back and thinks of the past,
Sighs her last sigh,
And slowly she dies.

Robin Watkins (11) Maldon Court School

BOOKS

I love to read books every day,
They could be about a seaside or a bay.
I get so involved I can't put them down,
whether they're about ballet or a clown.
I like to read when it is calm and peaceful,
when no-one's charging about like a bull,
When no-one shouts or calls.
I love to read books every day,
They could be about a seaside or a bay.

Laura Patience (10) Plumberow Primary School

MY FEELINGS ON A BIG WHEEL

When I climb in,
It starts shaking.
And as it goes round
And stops at the ground
You can't see anything
But when it goes high
I'd say goodbye
To my stomach
As it disappears.
But it's fun in a way.
It makes you say
Yippee
Hooray
This is great
For it goes round,
And round
Touch the ground
Then back you fly
Touch the sky
Very high
For it's fun
But when it's done
You walk out on the plank,
And feel like you
Have won a bank.

Lauren Pang (11) Plumberow Primary School

THE BIG WHEEL

On we get
You're scared I bet
We're going up again
That boy in front
He's higher than us
This really isn't fair
One more turn
And we're at the top
That boy is turning green
I'm at the top
And the ride has stopped
This always happens to me
Oh no it's stuck
I really must go down
I've been here hours I think
I really need a drink
Ah we finally go down
Look there's the village
And there's the town
But this is worse than going up
I think I feel like throwing up
At last we're nearly down
One more turn and we'll be there
At last we're going down again
Oh no we're going up and up
I'm at the top and going down
This really isn't so bad
We're at the bottom now
I'm glad it's over
I'm glad I'm down.

David Reid (11) Plumberow Primary School

SEALS

Swirling, diving
and splashing around.
Moving all different ways.
Upside down,
on their sides,
Turning, twisting
gliding and curling.
Making noises like,
Clowns' hooters!
What do they feel?
Do they think we're real?
All these faces looking at them,
Every day. Do they like it?

Jennifer Stratford (11) Plumberow Primary School

THE MORNING OF MY BIRTHDAY

I wake up in the morning
and hear the postman knock,
I go a running down the stairs
and undo the little lock,
There stands a great big parcel
with brightly coloured wrap,
I run into the living room and
put it on my lap,
I tear the paper off so fast
so everyone can see,
What's inside that parcel
that was addressed to me.

Jody Lacey (11) Plumberow Primary School

PE

I dread PE
I come into class and look at my PE bag
hanging helplessly on my peg.
I think, let me be ill or break my leg.
I get onto the field with my friends, they have
beaming smiles,
I bet I have a dark frown on mine.
'Kick your leg up,' the teacher bellowed at me.
I kicked up then dug my heel in the mud.
'OK everyone line up,' the teacher barked.
I stood near the back - I did not want to jog.
'Three laps' said the teacher with a wicked
smile.
Looking at the field I felt like being sick.
Got to the second lap my throat burning up,
My legs weak.
Finally I got to the end - '2.36' yelled the teacher.
Thank goodness it's over!

Lisa Candler (11) Plumberow Primary School

MY UGLY SISTER

My sister is called Emma,
She fights me every day,
If there was an ugly
Competition she's surely going
To win.

My sister is called Emma,
She is a horrible terror,
She takes my toys
And hides them,
So I hide hers.

Daniel Bacon (8) Plumberow Primary School

THE TEST

When I have a test
I look at my best friend
He looks petrified.
My hand is shaking like a leaf in a gale.
The teacher says, 'Hurry up.'
My face is as white as snow.
The first question is being read out,
I feel like being sick.
'9x8' the teacher bellowed.
Then my lead snapped.
I got my pencil sharpener
And scuttled over to the bin.
'Come on Chris,' the teacher says
My face now as red as blood
We're up to question 10 now
Nearly marking time.
Now I go all relaxed
I gave my book for someone to mark
My friend now as cool as ice
My book is given back
10 out of 10
Wow!

Chris Jude (10) Plumberow Primary School

HEATING

H ow do we get our power?
E verybody knows.
A nd yet not everybody realises,
T hat there are dangers, like,
I f you touch a plug with wet hands,
N o doubt you will be in hospital!
G raceful prayers being said for you.

Michael Fuller (11) Plumberow Primary School

OCEANS

The salty water glistening in the sun,
Whales swimming together,
Coming to the surface to breathe.
Dolphins swimming, diving out of the water,
Talking to each other,
Swimming near the bottom,
Investigating new places which haven't been
explored before.
The waves crashing against the rocks,
White foam sprays up into the air, then disappears.
Seals lying in the sun, on rocks, really still,
Just lying there until the blue water sweeps them
into it,
Swimming to get back to another rock.
The seaweed swaying with the current,
Some are green, some are brown,
Staying in the ground,
Until the current rips them out.
They slowly surface to the top.
On the beach, people sunbathing,
The sand, hot, because of the sun, but soft.
The crabs walking around in and out of the sea,
Their claws clipping things which they can't get hold
of,
Night comes -
Everybody goes.
Everything calm on the surface -
but not underneath.

David Wederell (11) Plumberow Primary School

OCEANS

Waves hurl themselves high in the air,
They grip for the sky.
But crashing back down to the sea.
Waves crashing, churning up the swirling sea,
They jump up at the sharp, stinging rocks,
Only to be hurled off.
The wind comes from high in the sky,
Stabbing the sea in the back.
The sea lets out a sharp wailing sound, of pain.
Black clouds are starting to darken,
Looking like black coal.
Rain starts to pour,
It blends with the wind.
The rain and wind flings itself at the sharp
rocks and the churning sea.
Rocks repel the stinging rain and the propelling
wind.
The clouds start to turn a tint of grey.
Monstrous sea, thrusting wind, alarming rain, are
starting to calm down.
The crashing waves no more,
Things start to quieten.
Now only the sound of the seagulls can be heard.

Hannah Wilhelmy (11) Plumberow Primary School

SISTERLY LOVE

My sister is sometimes nice
But at other times
She can be a pain in the neck
When she's nice
She plays with me
But when she's horrible
She makes a mess in my room
When it was tidy
And I get the blame
She tells lies about me
And I don't like it.

James Michael (7) Plumberow Primary School

BROTHER V SISTER

When my friend comes round,
My sister is always interfering with my games,
She is an absolute pain,
When she's in a mood I can't even speak to her!
It's true,
But she can be nice,
When we go shopping
She's popping up at all the toy shops
Hoping for a toy but I don't,
It's true.

Simon Darby (8) Plumberow Primary School

MY ANNOYING SISTER

My sister is so horrible,
She always annoys me,
She plays the piano when I'm watching TV
I shout for mum to tell her off,
But I get told off for shouting,
She grins at me, I grin back,
She hits me, I hit her,
But mum sees me, so I get the blame.

Lara Docking (9) Plumberow Primary School

MY SISTER IS A HORROR

My sister is horrid,
She scratches me,
She is the worst
Sister in the world.
When my friends
Come round,
She always is horrid.
But when she is sweet
She is really, really nice.

Emma Bagshaw (8) Plumberow Primary School

MY SISTER IS A PAIN IN THE NECK

My sister is a pain in the neck.
She ruins my toys.
She always takes my books when I am reading.
She lies all the time.
I always get the blame.
When her room is messy she said it was me
My sister is a pain in the neck
She can be nice sometimes.

Michelle Frampton (8) Plumberow Primary School

MY ANNOYING SISTER LOUISE

Louise my sister is very annoying.
When I am watching TV,
Louise is playing her clarinet,
To get her back,
I move her to the bedroom,
To have a fight with her.

When I make my bed,
My sister mucks it up again,
I get very angry
So I muck up hers!

Sophie Adams (9) Plumberow Primary School

SHOPPING

I go shopping with my mum
Lovely food scrummy yum yum.

Chicken, potatoes and all kinds of things
Soup and carrots and onion rings.

Gateway, Safeway all kinds of places
Loads of food and lots of faces.

Get to the checkout so how much is it?
My mum's about to have a fit.

Katie Smith (11) Plumberow Primary School

A BATTERY

B anging against the walls,
A nxious to get out,
T here lies some electric
T rying to get about!
E nraged by being trapped!
R efusing to stay in,
Y ou must be careful of him
because you might get zapped.

Paul Raven (11) Plumberow Primary School

MY FIRST GOAL

I remember it well, my first goal,
The ball came across,
And there I was unmarked.
Thud!
It hit my head,
The ball seemed to float in,
Goal everyone shouted.
The ref blew his whistle,
'End of the match' he said.
The manager came over,
'Great goal son,
Shame it was in our goal!'

Aaron Webb (11) Plumberow Primary School

SEAFRONT POEM

I'm riding along the seafront in my car,
With my mother and my brother, my father and all.
When we get out there we find a parking space,
When I get out the car, I say 'Hey this is the place!'
I'm sitting in a deckchair
Looking at fish
And I have got a load of ice-cream in a dish
I've only got one more wish,
And that's to be on the seafront 'Yeah!'

David Sains (11) Plumberow Primary School

THE BIG WHEEL

Up the top
Feeling greener by
The second.
Swaying to and fro.
People crying out loud.
Look at the view
I've lost my hat.
Don't look down.
Help I've got my leg stuck in the seat.
Get me off or I will sue you.
You can't from all the way up there.
It's going up again.
Can you feel the seaside air in your face.
Is it safe to be up here.
We're on the move again.
It feels like we're flying.
In the air like birds.
It's very slow.
Coming down.
Can I go on
Again.

James Irvine (10) Plumberow Primary School

THE EARTH AND THE MOON

On the earth you can hear the rustling wind,
The noise of cars,
The rain and hail in the puddles
And the sound of people walking.
On the moon all you can hear is the occasional noise of a rocket,
And yourself walking on the moon.

The earth has many different kinds of
animals, trees, buildings, fields, roads, streams and rivers.
On the moon you are surrounded by smokey grey rocks,
sand, dust and craters.

On the earth you can smell so many lovely things like
flowers, smoke, mint, damp soil and rain.
The moon does not have a smell.

The earth is dark blue, pondish green, sandy yellow and
cloudy white.
The moon is very dull and grey and sometimes silver.

The earth has many things to touch like bark, fruit, snow,
grass, rubber and paper.
On the moon you can feel rocks, sand and craters.

Mary Boursnell (10) Quilters Junior School

THE DRAGON

A dragon looks like a dinosaur
With lots of fat slimy scales
His eyes are like footballs
He has a head as big as a shed
And a mouth like a crocodile
That breaths out fire

His voice sounds like thunder
As he comes tearing through the clouds
And as he comes roaring
He shows his sharp fangs

Each step makes an earthquake
He barbecues everything in his way
He crushes trees and houses
He lives in a castle on a mountain

He only comes out at night
At night with eyes alight
He hunts for food.

Amy Fraser (8) Quilters Junior School

THE EARTH AND MOON

On the earth there are smells,
Like the lemon mint and mint leaves,
There's the smell of the classroom,
Old books, roses and best of all
  Sunday roast.

But on the moon it's scentless,
  Just the faint smell of humans,

The earth is surrounded by hills
And mountains,
                grass,
                         corn and
                                      buildings.

Out on the moon there's rock dust,
  The solar system,
Deep holes craters and gases
  Really it's just dead.

Natalie Moody (9) Quilters Junior School

SOMEWHERE

Out there somewhere way out in space,
There's a planet called mother Earth,
Where you and I stand in place,
It has countries and islands surrounded by the unique
blue sea.
The earth has a ball of rock and dust,
This ball by name is none other but the great almighty moon
On the moon it is silent the atmosphere is cold and numb,
All you can do is hear yourself breathe,
And the thumping of your heart,
The Earth is not so peaceful,
It's all so loud with people screaming,
And running all around,
And the noisy hoots from traffic,
but stop there hold on,
the Earth has got some good,
I like the sweet smell of roses,
The grass christened wet with dew,
The damp trees left over from the showery autumn
nights,
And the shiny brown conkers burst free from their
prickly green shells.

Naomi Embury (10) Quilters Junior School

THE EARTH AND THE MOON

The earth is a watery planet with one third
of it as land
But the moon is very different with caves
and rocks and sand.
Compared to the earth the moon is very
bare,
But the earth has trees and grass
everywhere.
The moon is not very colourful with
smoky grey and dusty brown
The earth is completely different with
yellows, blues and greens all round and
round.
The clouds on earth are wispy white the sea
a murky blue
The moon is like a black and white film
Not the place for me or you.
On the moon you will feel rocks going
beneath your feet
On earth the grass all tidy and neat.
On the moon you can see all the planets
and stars
While on earth you can only see Venus,
Jupiter and Mars
In space there is nothing to eat
I'm glad I'm not on the moon!

Anita Gupta (10) Quilters Junior School

VE DAY MEMORY

When father left I was only six.
Five years later I am no longer a little girl at eleven.
Everyone was very worried about him.
I remember I cried a lot when he left.

All of us were overjoyed when we heard he was coming home.
He would be arriving on the six o'clock from Paddington.
It was a long way to the station so we set out early with high hearts
and hopes.
We arrived tired but still jubilant.

We waited on the platform for what must have been ten minutes but
seemed like hours.
As the train pulled in happy, joyful expressions came over the faces of
the people waiting, for the first time in ages.
I rushed to the first door that opened, none of the men
who walked out looked like father.
I ran from door to door as they opened but did not see father.
I heard mother's voice calling me back.
With a heavy heart I slowly walked back to her.

Just before I reached mother I took a last look back down the station.
I spotted a familiar face scarred and changed by the pain of war, but
still father.
I dashed towards him through all the other people's arms outstretched.
We embraced.
I burst into tears I was so happy.
Mother spotted him, stood mouth open for a moment and then
followed me.

The War is over!

Alison Bateman (10) Quilters Junior School

BULLET

Bullet, bang,
There it goes,
In the air,
It can't stop,
Pointed, long
Dangerous to you
Never know what
It is going to do,
Maybe
It will shoot
Right through
Maybe
It will kill you

Fiona McCluskey (10) St Alban's RC JMI School, Hornchurch

GOING ON HOLIDAY

Going on holiday,
Is when you have some fun,
playing in the swimming pool,
and annoying your mum.
Saying,
'Can I have an ice-cream,
Can I have an ice-cream,
Yes, yes, yes, yes, yes.'
Well my mum was wrong,
and I was right.
But I'm going to have more fun
Tonight.

Yvonne West (8) St Alban's RC JMI School, Hornchurch

ONCE I WOKE UP

Once I woke up on a Sunday morn
and found red spots on the garden lawn.
I went to tell my mum, I said,
'Come on wake up you sleepy head!'
I told my dad, my brother too.
The cheetah must have lost them from the zoo.
So we all went off to the zoo surprised.
My dad, mum, brother and I.

Sarah Fissler (10) St Alban's RC JMI School, Hornchurch

BORED

I'm really bored,
Anything you say I have done.
I've scared the cat,
And I've killed my sister's dolls.

I pulled their hair,
I've pulled their eyes out.
I've hung them up by the neck,
And chucked them in the bin.

Can't you see I'm bored?
I'm like a bear wild with rage
I want to go back to school,
Can't you see I'm
      Bored!

James Willoughby (10) St Alban's RC JMI School, Hornchurch

FANTASY FOOTBALL

I get the ball
Run with it
Off down the pitch
Shoot goal
England one
The rest of the world one
Only ten seconds to go,
Here comes young Potts
Past two
Past two more
And another two
and that's six
Goal keeper isn't glad.

Danny Franklin (11) St Alban's RC JMI School, Hornchurch

GIRLS

Girls are babies
They always suck their thumbs.
They always chat
And even scream.
They always scratch
And even squeal.
I'm glad I'm a boy

Ross Francis (9) St Alban's RC JMI School, Hornchurch

AN OBJECT

There's a box on my table
I can't really see
What's inside
What can it be
I open the lid
To see what's inside
I see a bullet
Long and wide
Pointed on the top
I think it is a pretty box
Long, short
And as still as can be
The bullet's
Inside
So it wouldn't
Kill me.

Laura Osborn (10) St Alban's RC JMI School, Hornchurch

FLYING

One day at the park
I was swinging on a big swing
I went higher and higher
And I let go
I went flying through the air
I saw Mars, Jupiter and went past Australia
When I came in to land
Everyone was clapping and cheering

Mary Munson (11) St Alban's RC JMI School, Hornchurch

NOISES AT NIGHT

There's a monster under my bed
Waiting quietly for me to put my foot down
That's my first fear

Then the patting of the rain
Like a ghost trying to get in
That's scary too.

The creeping of the water going through the
pipes
Like a robber moving in the house
Very creepy.

I hear the hooting of owls
In the night time trees.

Billy Calvert (10) St Alban's RC JMI School, Hornchurch

NOISES AT NIGHT

One night in bed
In a new house
I hear noises
Like trees about to break
I also hear drain pipes,
Will one come off
And hit the floor?
I look out of the window
It's only the slide in the garden
The swing is swinging
Backwards and forwards.

Tony Humphreys (10) St Alban's RC JMI School, Hornchurch

THE SEA

The sea is coming to me from an angle it is cold
It is trickling up my legs like a crab on a wall
Something has risen out of the sea and it is a
beautiful baby seal
He suddenly jumped out of the sea
It is very very pretty and has lovely white fur
It is now coming on to the beach
It has come up to me and cuddled me.

Lucy Cannon (11) St Alban's RC JMI School, Hornchurch

I SPEND MY TIME

When I am at home I have plenty to do
I go to the shops and sometimes the zoo.
I visit my gran's and my cousins too,
There is always something different and new.
When we stay home I play with my toys
With all my friends, both girls and boys.
We play in the garden, we play in the shed
Often until it's time for bed.
My time at home is lots of fun
Busy and happy 'till the day is done.

Charlotte Thacker (10) St Alban's RC JMI School, Hornchurch

STEVE BULL

Steve Bull,
Is so cool,
He is the best at football.
He scores goals,
Good ones too,
The boots he wears,
Are really new.
The songs about him,
Are never dim.
One of the songs goes like this
'Oh!
Bully is a tatter,
He wears an England cap,
He plays for Wolverhampton,
And he's a lucky chap.
He scores with his left foot, he scores with his right,
And when we play the Albion, he'll score a few all right.'

Daniel Kelly (10) St Alban's RC JMI School, Hornchurch

WORMS

Worms are wiggly,
And slimy all over.
They eat lots of leaves,
Like a four leaf clover.
They live underground,
And they roll around
They're so quiet,
They never make a sound.

Alex Campbell (11) St Alban's RC JMI School, Hornchurch

MY GHOST

There's a ghost in my bedroom
I really like him
One night he took me to the moon
And then he said
'We will go back soon'

Now he's gone
I'm very sad
but then mum said
'There's a ghost in the bedroom'
And now he's *come back!*

Mark O'Connell (10) St Alban's RC JMI School, Hornchurch

SCHOOL MEMORIES

I started school one September
Still I can remember
The first day at school.
All the teachers seemed so tall.

Now I'm Year Six
And I'm not so small
So the teachers don't seem that tall.

Lindsay Madden (10) St Alban's RC JMI School, Hornchurch

WHAT IS IN THE AIR?

I am flying through the air,
The wind blowing in my face.
It's a sunny day with a lovely sky,
And nice white clouds.
As I go by I pass aeroplanes,
The passengers wave at me,
I wave back.
I also pass birds they sing and flutter as they go by
It's a wonderful experience, flying through the air,
It kind of makes you feel like forgetting all your worries
And is like a world where there are no worries,
And is always happy
When I got home my Mum said 'Patrick where have you been?'
I didn't answer,
And walked quietly to my room.

Patrick Cannon (11) St Alban's RC JMI School, Hornchurch

NEW SCHOOL

My hopes and fears of all the years are
finally coming true.
I'm going to my Secondary School
And I have to buy my clothes, all new.

I'll have to work very hard because
this is the school that really matters.
In a way I don't want to go
But I know
I have to go
I'm sure it will turn out
All right in the end.

Louise Meehan (11) St Alban's RC JMI School, Hornchurch

THE ZOO

My best friend and I went to the zoo
We saw the elephants and monkey too.

I think the dolphins are the best
But I really enjoyed all the rest.

Time goes by when you're having fun
It didn't matter that we didn't see the sun.

The time went by as quick as a flash
When it got dark we had to dash.

When we got home I dreamt of the zoo
I dreamt of the monkeys and the elephants too.

Ciara Honeyball (1) St Alban's RC JMI School, Hornchurch

MOANING MUM

My mum's a real bad moaner
She moans at my family and I.
She screams and shouts in our earholes
I feel like I'm going to die.

She moans about anything she can think of
Moans about this and about that.
She moans that my sister's too skinny
She moans that my dad is too fat.

But mum is my mum
Even though she is a pain.
She's not that bad a moaner
Oh, here she goes again.

Lauren Eames (11) St Alban's RC JMI School, Hornchurch

SECONDARY SCHOOLS

Of all the fears of all the years
Most of them come now
Off to a new school.
But it's going to be cool.

I'm going to feel small in that tall
tall building.
I'm going to be on my own
I'll try not to moan or groan
When the bell goes I'll feel like I've
been in a shell.
When I get home I dread the next day.

Kevin Quinlan (10) St Alban's RC JMI School, Hornchurch

DEAD OF NIGHT

The dead of night the dead of night
gives me such an awful fright.
I go to bed fast
because I don't want to be haunted by ghosts from the past.
I try to stay awake but
I fall asleep.
I wake up and stare at the morning light.

Liam Tegart (11) St Alban's RC JMI School, Hornchurch

STONE

Cold,
Hollow,
Bumpy.
Dull colours,
Patterns inside,
Sitting on table.
Quietly still.

Looks like a bear
Holes look like
Eyes and ears
Bumps like ears and nose
Makes me feel cold.

Caroline Upward (11) St Alban's RC JMI School, Hornchurch

AUSCHWITZ POEM

Yesterday they brought me here, brought
Me here to die,
They said they'd give me food and clothes
All that was a lie.
The clothes are light and cold gets through
Innocents die with nothing to do.

I am a child ten years old
I used to be both strong and bold
I'm now a baby cold and weak
The future itself looks dark and bleak.

Children weak and cold and ill
Rumours spreading that showers kill
We are young and slowly dying
It's no use sitting down and crying.

Anthony McShea (10) St Antony's RC School, Woodford Green

I WILL SURVIVE

I am a Jew it is true
Hitler hates us why is this true
If he finds us we will be killed
    I am a Jew it is true.

Life is hard no fun no games
    So hard it's true
But I am still a Jew
We hide all day with no food to eat
And I try to say all day
'Everything is fine, no problems we
won't die.'
    Is this true
    I am a Jew
    I am just like you.

Lucy Morgan (11) St Antony's RC School, Woodford Green

BEHIND THE WIRE

Here I am behind the wire,
in this place that I don't
know.

More people here by the
hour, screaming, shouting, I
don't know why

I just do my jobs in
the work house, every
day.

Luck is coming right
my way.

They asked if I wanted
a shower, I said
'Yes' so I'm going today.

Laura Parkinson (10) St Antony's RC School, Woodford Green

HOW AM I GOING TO SURVIVE?

I woke up in the morning
Feeling blue.

I said to myself
What am I going to do?

I'm in hiding, hoping and trying
All my family are really lying,

If we are found,
We'll go to a concentration ground.

All the way down the line
I hope my family are fine.

I hope my friend has not died
How am I going to survive?

Lucy-Anne Wartnaby (11) St Antony's RC School, Woodford Green

POOR

Poor as I am I do survive.

Each morning I wake up,
each morning I take up,
the feeling of frustration.

I sit on the street
with dirty and wet feet
watching the posh people pass.
I hold out my hand
waiting for someone to understand
my feeling of distress.

At midnight
when my feelings are tight
I might pay a visit to the market.
And there I hide
the dark lamps behind
eating scraps of food.

And then I meet
the other children
who live their lives on the street.

Shanthini Crusz (10) St Antony's RC School, Woodford Green

THE WORLD THAT I WANT

I want a world where peace is free,
Where we can live in harmony.
Where women are treated with some respect,
and children can be free from poverty.
Bombs, that's what they make,
They have no choice they must give and take!
I wish one day that I could say,
Every face is bonny and gay!

I want a world where happiness is everything,
Where people can live in a friendship ring.
Where men are not forced to die,
and women at home don't have to cry!
Where it is safe to go outside at night,
and all the wrong is forever put right.
I wish one day that I could say
It's peace at last, war has gone away!

Catherine Mahon (11) St Antony's RC School, Woodford Green

THE BIGGEST ROCKET

Shining shimmering
dark and bright,
spitting and fizzing
all through the night.
The jumping flames dance on the fire,
the Catherine Wheel
was my desire.

The rockets jump and
shoot into the night,
we have to make sure
the time is right,
for the biggest rocket
there and then,
don't go near it
be careful, Ben!

>   Whoosh! Bang! Eeow!
>   It's gone! It's gone!
>   Oh no! Oh no!
>   All that is left are
>   ashes and bone.

Hannah Ryder (11) St Hilda's School, Westcliffe-on-Sea

THE LISTENER

He rode out of the valley
To a place unknown
His horse was kicking up
the dust
And he felt quite alone.
He closed his eyes
And smelt the air,
And to his surprise
A man was there.
The moonlit sky had now appeared
He knew he was the listener.
He stopped and froze with fear.
'Are you the listener?'
The young man called,
'I was supposed to meet him here.'
'I am not the one you want,
Go home and don't come back.
The listener went thirty years ago.'
The young man felt very sad.
I shall go now,
Never come back,
Never.
He put his foot upon the stirrup,
And rode towards the valley.
The listener has gone he said to himself,
The listener has gone forever.

Jessica Lucey (11) St Hilda's School, Westcliff-on-Sea

IT'S THE MORNING OF THAT DAY

It's the morning of that day.
That very same day.
That this time last year,
Stole my friend away.

It's the morning of that day,
Where rockets fly high.
I just cannot believe,
The way time flies by.

It's the morning of that day.
The day where people say.
'Be safe around fireworks,
Don't give your life away!'

It's the morning of that day,
When my friend got hurt.
It was really nasty,
To watch her being burnt.

It's the morning of that day,
That very same day.
That this time last year,
Stole my friend away.

Sophie Hunt (11) St Hilda's School, Westcliff-on-Sea

BARN OWL

How wise your deep brown eyes are.
How soft your speckled wings.
When I see you gliding,
like a great white moth,
I think of such beautiful things.
Magic and mystery and wonderful thoughts,
as you glide in the silver starlight.
With you up there in the moonlit air
you make it a beautiful night.

Katharine Davies (9) St Hilda's School, Westcliff-on-Sea

THE SEA

The sea and its colours are dull and bright.
They change all the time whenever they like.
The colours are different each and every one,
silver, grey, emerald, blue.
The water is cold nearly all the time.
I look for my favourite shell,
which looks like a rolled up piece of paper.
Most are broken, some are pretty.
On cold days like this,
it's not very pleasant to swim in the sea.
But on warm days in summer,
it's good to keep cool.
So go for a swim if you want to keep cool.

Lara Cardosi (11) St Hilda's School, Westcliff-on-Sea

DOGS

My dog has a really long tail,
A really big nose,
A really happy smile,
My dog is as tall as my knee,
His lick is so soft,
He has a really soft head,
My dog follows me wherever I go,
Does whatever I say
He has two big floppy ears,
My dog has a patch on one eye,
He's black and white,
His name is Timmy,
But we call him Tim for short,
My dog has water to drink
And has meat to eat,
My dog is my best friend,
And when I go to sleep he lays on my feet.

Amy Tetchner (10) St Hilda's School, Westcliff-on-Sea

THE SEA

Sometimes the sea is like glass
Sometimes the sea is rough like a tiger
Looking out of my window
I see windsurfers,
Fishermen,
People painting,
Little children collecting shells,
Making sand castles.
I see the ice-cream man
Selling lollies and soft ice-cream.

Later in the evening
I watch the sea, so still,
No movement at all.
Big tankers locked up
Yachts swaying on their moorings,
Fishing boats drifting
As far as they can go.
Peaceful 'till the next tide.

Victoria Hamme (11) St Hilda's School, Westcliff-on-Sea

FIREWORK DAY

Stand well back!
Here it goes!
Where it goes no-one knows,
Shining lights of all different colours
Children with babies, babies with mothers.
The Catherine Wheel spins round and round
Ashes from sparklers fall to the ground
The Roman Candle lets off a bang
It's just as noisy as a tram.
The bonfire starts,
The guy is lit
All dead sparklers are put in a pit,
The last firework comes out of the box,
The bonfire's caused an enormous fog.
Oh no, there's the dog!
The last firework is lit
And goes with a woosh,
Jenny don't push
The firework goes into the air
And bursts into different colours.

Sarah Parmenter (11) St Hilda's School, Westcliff-on-Sea

THE BIG FIGHT

It's the fight of the season
between Spring and Winter
In Spring it's the blossom,
daffodil and camellia.

        Then on to Winter
        that's the snowy season
        with snowdrops and wind
        It's completely bare of blossom.

The fight has begun
and it's Winter in the lead
but Spring's here with new lambs
and lots of tangy marmalade.

        Which one will win?
        I hope it's not Winter
        it's cold and wet
        and the wet wood gives me splinters.

I think Spring's coming back
yes, here he is with all his flowers
Spring's now on track
With gardeners cutting the grass with their mowers.

        Spring's now won!
        Hooray, Hooray!
        feel the warmth of the sun!
        Hip, Hip Hooray!

Amy Cockell (11) St Hilda's School, Westcliff-on-Sea

SHROVE TUESDAY

Here we come, we are all awake.
We are ready for a pancake.
Mummy's tossing them,
We are watching them,
bit by bit,
one by one
Even, in a bun
'Whoops-a-daisy'
Mummy's gone crazy!
It's landed on our cat Maisy.

Hollie Bunker (10) St Hilda's School, Westcliff-on-Sea

RAIN

I gazed through the window,
I looked at the ground
Big puddles lying all around.
The rain came down from the sky,
Making the puddles rise up very high.
I got my wellies and grabbed my coat,
Then went into the garden which looked like a moat.
I jumped in the puddles,
In and out,
Splashing the water all about.
I laughed in glee,
I was as happy as can be.

Laura Hurley (10) St Hilda's School, Westcliff-on-Sea

THE NYMPH

I was walking in the forest one night
When I saw a big blue light,
I got such a fright
When I saw it was a nymph!
She had a pink scruffy dress
That looked a bit of a mess.
She was about six centimetres high
And I am not telling a lie!
She was searching for pollen inside a rose
When a bit got up my nose.
By accident I sneezed
She turned around in fright,
And vanished with her big blue light.

Hannah Sheridan (10) St Hilda's School, Westcliff-on-Sea

A CHRISTMAS POEM

C hristmas is here it is fun to play at Christmas in the snow.
H olly is pretty when you put your decorations up.
R eindeers - I can see Rudolph upon the roof top.
I can see Santa on the roof, Santa is coming to our house today.
S anta's coming today I wonder what toys I will get.
T insel - I like putting tinsel on the Christmas tree.
M erry Christmas everyone.
A dvent is a lovely time to get ready for Christmas.
S now - we can play in the snow today.

Leanne Linwood (8) St Joseph the Worker RC Primary School, Hutton

IT'S A CATERPILLAR'S LIFE

A Caterpillar is crawling up
my leg,
I can feel all ten legs.
Ho! Hee! How it tickles.

There is goes up that tree.
Quick let's follow it.
What's it doing?
It's turning into something.
Ben it's bedtime!
Coming Mum!
zzzzzzzzzzzzzzzzz

Good Morning.
I've just looked at the Caterpillar
and there's no sign of life.
Come and see.

Look it's moving.
Now it's opening.
Look at that
It's so beautiful and
colourful.
It's yellow, red, pink and orange.

Off it goes.
Up and up and up
and now it's gone.
'Bye I have to go now.'

Max Ward (8) St Joseph the Worker RC Primary School, Hutton

THE SIGHT OF SPRING

Spring is a beautiful time of year
the flowers are flowering and the trees
are getting leaves.
I can go outside and see the sight of spring
Spring is a beautiful time of year.
I can go and pick the beautiful flowers
Spring is a beautiful time of year.
The sight of spring of beautiful.

Hannah Harrison-Griffiths (8) St Joseph the Worker RC Primary School, Hutton

THE BLOSSOM OF THE SPRING

In the springtime the blossom hangs on the trees,
some become fruit and some stay blossom.
I love the spring in the blossom!
Little raindrops hang on the blossom, as I walk past.
I see the glitter of the blossom
with the raindrops hanging
down.

Nicole Vella (8) St Joseph the Worker RC Primary School, Hutton

THE DAY THAT IT WAS AUTUMN

The day that it was autumn we said
What should we do today? Throw leaves
far away? As you see them go by you think
You want to say 'goodbye', but you
can't because they haven't got ears so they
can't hear.

The day that it was autumn we said what
should we do today. It's not winter so we
can't make a snowman. It's not spring so
you can't have Easter eggs. It's not summer
so we can't sunbathe. So what should we
do? I know, I know, we can throw leaves around.

Jack Maloney (8) St Joseph the Worker RC Primary School, Hutton

THE VIKING SHIP SAILS

The Viking ship sails.
Wind whistling, waves crashing
Thunder crashing. Adventures growing
Sea getting in your eyes and
getting annoyed too. And then

    Splash! A Wave

Helen Davey (8) St Joseph the Worker RC Primary School, Hutton

VIKE SPEED

Speeding through the splashing waves
With the strong current trying to push
you back.
Suddenly you see some rocks.
You try to dodge them,
But *wham!*
You went bump into a rock.
Then you hear a *crash!* In the sky,
And you look up
It was lightning.
Then thunder started pouring down.
Suddenly you hear 'crack.'
You look at the boat.
You see the boat cracking
and then *splash*!
You go deep down into the sea.

Mary-Louise Smith (8) *St Joseph the Worker RC Primary School, Hutton*

THE SUN

The sun is round the sun is bright.
The sun is warm on you. The sun is a
fireball. The sun is made of a lot of
gases. You can sunbathe, be careful
that you do not get sunburnt.
Did you know the sun was made for you?

Lucy Turnbull (8) *St Joseph the Worker RC Primary School, Hutton*

THE GARDEN

Garden, garden
Why are you so long?
With beautiful flowers and roses too,
Trees as well.
Nice beautiful garden.

Daisies too.
The thing in this garden I like
Is everything.

Ciaran Kehoe (8) St Joseph the Worker RC Primary School, Hutton

CATERPILLAR CATERPILLAR CATERPILLAR CRAWL

Caterpillar Caterpillar big and small.
Caterpillar Caterpillar you have a
lovely crawl.
Caterpillar Caterpillar having a dig.
Caterpillar Caterpillar crawling on a
twig.
Caterpillar Caterpillar eating all
summer.
Caterpillar Caterpillar wake up in a
beautiful colour.

Matthew Hooper (8) St Joseph the Worker RC Primary School, Hutton

PEACE AND FREEDOM

War is really bad,
War is really sad,
It mucks up the life which you used
to have.

War is not good,
it never should . . .
go ahead

I wish war was dead,
It goes to your head.
Peace and Freedom rule.

May 7th
more bombs fall,
May 8th,
bombs of Peace and Freedom fall,
Peace and Freedom really rule.

Andrew Haswell (10) St Lawrence School, Rowhedge

WHAT PEACE AND FREEDOM MEANS TO ME

War is dumb, War is dim.
War does not mean anything to me.
War is bad, War is sad
Hope Hitler goes to hell.
War is dumb, War is dim
If it happens again I don't
Want to be here.

Lee Saunders (11) St Lawrence School, Rowhedge

WHAT PEACE AND FREEDOM MEANS TO ME

Peace is a precious thing to me.
I live in freedom and I want to
stay that way.
Peace is important because if we
don't have peace we will always
be fighting and killing people.
Freedom means to me, running and
playing and having fun with my
friends.
Why can't the world live in peace
all together peacefully.

Sophie Fincham (11) St Lawrence School, Rowhedge

WHAT PEACE AND FREEDOM MEANS TO ME

Peace to me is no more war, no more
guns, no more nuclear wars. Why can't
anybody live in peace any more? Why can't
we say goodbye to it all? I want to say
goodbye to it all. There's no need for it all.
There's no Freedom either for me because I'm at
school, why can't we be free?

Adam Thrower (11) St Lawrence School, Rowhedge

PEACE AND FREEDOM

Freedom is very special to this
world. No-one should die in
a horrid way. Freedom is to
lose a war or to win. War
doesn't exist any more
People celebrated when
the war was over, so there
was peace at last.
Hitler put the world in ruins
but we stopped him for
peace.

Ian Vickery (10) St Lawrence School, Rowhedge

PEACE AND FREEDOM

Let there be peace as it is in heaven.
Let the world hear you speaking. Stop
the world from war. We're so lucky.
There is no war so thank God for this
long happiness.

Dale Young (11) St Lawrence School, Rowhedge

SCHOOL

I live in Harlow, I live in
a house, I go to school
Without a doubt.
My mum says I'm too
brainy to go to school,
what does she *know*

Philomena Loughran (10) St Luke's RC Primary School, Harlow

SPRING

Winter has gone spring is here,
the sun is high the skies are clear.
The grass is green, flowers bloom,
fresh winds have blown away the gloom.

Vanessa Lewis (9) St Luke's RC Primary School, Harlow

THE BLESSING

Happy are you the old
for one day you will be young

Happy are you the lame
for one day you will walk

Happy are you the people of God
for you will never die.

Nathanael Ozanne (9) St Luke's RC Primary School, Harlow

I AM A PEST

I am a pest everybody says,
Because I stand in their way.
But nobody knows how I feel inside,
Since my great nan died.
Everybody argues with me,
And my mum sits me on her knee.
And tries to make it better,
But no-one can make it better.

I am a pest everybody says,
Because I stand in their way.
Deep down inside they all hate me,
And to them I'm like a bee.
Who follows them about and gets on their nerves,
And I'm never part of any of their herds.
I am a pest everybody says,
Just because I go my own way.

Claire O'Connor (11) St Luke's RC Primary School, Harlow

A MOUSE

I'd like to be a mouse so soft and small.
With a twitchy nose long, long tail.
I could be Mickey Mouse or a biker mouse.
I investigate mouse traps like Basil.
I'd have a lot of exercise getting chased by cats.
My babies would be all pink.
I'll make a nest to keep them warm.
I'll scamper to get my cheese.
I'll sca-rree people out of their houses.
Till my babies are mouses.

Matthew Jennings (11) St Luke's RC Primary School, Harlow

MY TORTOISE

My tortoise is a slow one,
and he's not very fast,
he goes out for long walks
and makes his dinner last.

My tortoise walks so slowly,
on his little paws,
munching at the grass,
with his little jaws.

He doesn't need a house,
a caravan or flat,
his shell is the home,
instead of all of that.

He'd love to be an eagle,
in the sky a-soaring,
the trouble is,
a tortoise's life is very very boring.

Victoria Humphreys (10) St Mary's Prittlewell CE Primary School
Southend-on-Sea

FOOTBALL

Football football it's such fun
The pitch is so big I like to run
At the end when the whistle blows it's all done
Hooray hooray our team has won
Then I go home with mum
For a burger in a bun.

Glenn Little (8) St Mary's Prittlewell CE Primary School
Southend-on-Sea

SHARING

The leaves on the trees,
The clouds in the sky,
The cows that make cheese,
The birds that can fly.

The things on the ground,
Some shapely and square,
Some make a nice sound,
For all of us to share.

Sizzling bacon under the grill,
The opened beans in a tin,
The great big bag of corn from the mill,
The empty cans in the bin.

Third world countries miss out on all this,
They languish and starve all day long,
If we only shared some of our bliss,
They too would be healthy and strong.

Think of those people without any food.
If we're not greedy,
They won't be needy!

Joanna Duckworth (10) St Mary's Prittlewell CE Primary School,
Southend-on-Sea

MY BROTHER

My brother's all happy and glad
He usually makes me mad
He's so happy all the time
Makes me happy that he's mine
That brother of mine

Dean Hanby (8) St Mary's Prittlewell CE Primary School
Southend-on-Sea

POG DOG 53

I play pog but not in the fog
'Cause you can't see what you're doing
So switch the light on please do dog
And kindly stop your booing
I like this game
I'm good at pog
I'm expert with the slammers
So kindly stop your booing dog
You should have better manners.

Sam Stone (8) St Mary's Prittlewell CE Primary School
Southend-on-Sea

BIG BAD BULLY

There is a big bully in our school.
And he really is quite bad.
His name is Michael McPool.
And he's driving me quite mad.

Every time I wake up.
I feel like I'm going to die.
I always try to make up.
But they always make me cry.

Every Monday I go to games.
They always pick on me.
They take the mickey, they call me names.
They always worry me.

My mum says I must ignore them.
Leave them right alone.
Even though I'm petrified.
I'm still, when I get home.

Louise Hodder (10) St Mary's Prittlewell CE Primary School
Southend-on-Sea

NEW SHOES

Today's the day
I'm off to buy my brand new shoes
I'm as excited as can be
Lots of shoes for me to see
Mum gives me clues
Will it be a pair with bows?
Or light pink with a tiny rose?
School shoes or party shoes
Disco dancing, tap shoes
Ouch! My feet must not bruise
I must be careful which pair I choose
Oh dear, mum gives a sigh
I'd better hurry and make my choice
Else I'll go home *without* my brand new shoes.

Fay Leese (8) St Mary's Prittlewell CE Primary School
                              Southend-on-Sea

THE GHOST HOUSE

Have you heard about the house down south?
It's a ghost house and it's got a door like a mouth,
It's got trapdoors, passages and stuff like that,
And when you open a closet out comes a bat.
Frankenstein's there and Dracula too,
and there's some monsters that should be in the zoo!
Skeletons coming out of coffins and stuff.
This is too scary I've had enough!

Daniel Lee Bishop (8) St Mary's Prittlewell CE Primary School,
                              Southend-on-Sea

PEOPLE

If you're white or coloured, together
we could help each other.
We should make friends and we should like
each other
Not hate each other because it is not right
We can all make a difference to help people
with disabilities
We could make this world a better place by
liking not hating.
Caring not ignoring, loving not hurting
and we should love animals more than
we do
So we can all make a difference starting
from now.
So go to school and we could learn all about
people
So we can help other people.

Lisa Jane Fowke (8) St Mary's Prittlewell CE Primary School
Southend-on-Sea

THE BIG FAT CRAB

When you go to the seaside,
Watch out, because the big
fat crab is about.
He walks, he bites, he swims
But worst of all the bite
Stings.

So when you go down to the
Seaside,
Watch out for the big fat crab!

Ciaran Finn (9) St Mary's RC Primary School, Tilbury

THE BOY WHO BANGED HIS HEAD

There was this boy who banged his head,
He said, 'Oh my I better go to bed.'
He fell asleep and had a dream,
And when he woke up he was in a stream.

The stream was long the stream was wide,
Then suddenly there came a massive big tide.
He said, 'Oh my what should I do?'
And he started to cry he said, 'Boo hoo.'

Then out of the sky there came a big bird,
Then another, then a third.
One picked him up they went so fast,
They saw his house but they went past.

The bird dropped him on the ground,
Then he heard a familiar sound.
He thought I've heard that sound before,
And then he remembered it was a knock
on the door.

Well we all know what that must mean,
It must have been a terrible dream.

Stephanie Kok (11) St Mary's RC Primary School, Tilbury

THE NEW LOOK

Have you heard about this new book
It's got a great new cover
And a great new look
It's got loads of pages
From children of all ages
You can read it and read it
Until you get bored of it
But please don't throw it away!

Charlotte Ager (10) St Mary's RC Primary School, Tilbury

WHAT I LIKE

I like a lot of jam,
  with my ham,
Custard,
  with a lot of mustard,
I like my steak,
  to be cut in the shape of cake,
For my rice,
  to be like ice,
For my stew,
  not to be like you,
My pie,
  just to be for I,
And my tea,
  to be just for me.

Mary Mcpherson (11) St Mary's RC Primary School, Tilbury

CHRISTMAS TIME

The bells are ringing
Angels are singing.
Santa Claus is coming
With all our presents,
The turkey is cooking
For our roast dinner.
Under the tree are presents
For you and for me.
Then we unwrapped our gifts
And prayed for joy
on Christmas day.

Chantelle Samba (8) St Mary's RC Primary School, Tilbury

A WORLD AT WAR

What use is a world at war with
anger and fighting forever more?
You see it everywhere on the TV
Why can't people see how peaceful the
world can really be
Peace is what the world needs
Not fighting and killing to be freed
You hear about war more each day
It looks like war is here to stay
As long as we have peace that's all
we need
And we can begin to plant a brand new
seed
A seed that is of hope and love
And gradually it will rise above this
war and disaster and hope that it
will last forever after
What use is a world at war with
anger and fighting forever more?

Hannah Walker (11) St Peter's CE Primary School, South Weald

GRAPES

Ripe green grapes hanging on the vines.
A special man who works there makes the grapes into wine,
People go and buy the wine.
The grown-ups say it tastes divine.
The grapes are very good for me.
When it's hot in the middle of May,
The grapes will refresh me in the middle of the day.
At harvest time people give and get,
That's what Harvest is all about

Ross Nicholson (11) St Peter's CE Primary School, South Weald

WHAT'S HAPPENING?

Winter has gone,
Spring has begun,
Buds appear
Once a year,
They form leaves
And grow on trees,
Flowers are born
By bulbs that aren't torn,
Animals return
To homes alone,
The snow melts away
And the grass is here today,
The crops grow,
And there's no more snow,
That's what happens in spring.

Adam Samuel (10) St Peter's CE Primary School, South Weald

WHAT'S HAPPENING

Birds are flying all around the
Park.
Getting pieces of mud, twig and bark
Young birds have their mouths open
Wide
While their parents are going
Outside to look for food to care
For their group.

The days are getting longer, the
Grass is growing too.
People are getting happier and trees
Are leaving blossoming too.

Chris Portou (11) St Peter's CE Primary School, South Weald

A POEM FOR PEACE

Peace is the word that means,
You're happy, joyful and full of beans,
When something has come to an end,
It could be a war or a fight with a friend.

Do people really need to fight,
It doesn't matter if you're black or white,
Guns, bombs and shelling is a painful thing,
In hope people pray and sing.

Children have to flee from their homes,
Leaving things he or she owns,
If nations agreed more,
I don't think there would be a war.

So please let's try to stop war
I thought that's what peace was for,
Whatever your colour, size or weight,
Stop all wars and our world would be great.

Helen Richardson (11) St Peter's CE Primary School, South Weald

WHAT'S HAPPENING?

It gets warmer well, we hope for the best.
The birds return and build nests,
Daylight lengthens new grass will grow,
Spring flowers everywhere it seems so slow.
Baby lambs are born,
Blossom is all over your garden lawn.
Buds are on the trees,
And soon there will be leaves.
Spring is here.

Ann Platt (10) St Peter's CE Primary School, South Weald

THE SUN

Sun so big, round and wide
You fill the sky with your beams
Of pride
The earth spins round right by your
Side.
You are the ruler of the sky.

July and August really must be
Your favourite time of year,
You beam your beams
Down on the sand
And watch the children playing
On the land.

Sun you beam your rays
With all your might
You're a great big yellow light
You're the light bulb of the sky,
Without you we would surely, surely
Die!

Claire Belson (10) St Peter's CE Primary School, South Weald

PEACE IN THE WORLD

War is a terrible thing,
Peace is great,
It helps us play, laugh and sing,
We need peace to keep us strong,
And keep us working all day long.

Tanks and guns are not the way,
But they go on all of the day,
People that suffer all the time
Really need to climb
To the top
And never stop.

If peace was around us now,
We would really know
How to be good and loyal,
Don't be nasty or cruel,
And that is the general rule.

Antony Lynn (11) St Peter's CE Primary School, South Weald

WHAT'S HAPPENING?

Birds
Build their nests,
And have some young.
The grass is green,
The babies are born,
And the flowers have come.

The days are getting longer,
The flowers' scent is getting stronger
People get happy.
Winter is gone, summer is to come.

Everybody is full of energy.
The rabbits hop around the field.
The wind is blowing,
The sun is shining,
And spring is all around.

Fiona Hornsby (10) St Peter's CE Primary School, South Weald

PEACE

Peace is something that is knocking at our door,
But to let it in,
We must stop the war.
People go out to kill,
Just think how their families feel.
The world is just one big place,
Peace is living together,
No matter your race.
Peace is loving enemies too,
Whoever you are,
Could I, could you?
If you could, there'd be no war,
Peace is something we want more and more.
It doesn't matter what your colour is,
Black or white,
It's still no reason for you to fight.
Peace is something that is knocking at our door,
But to let it in,
We must stop the war.

Carl Harvey (11) St Peter's CE Primary School, South Weald

THE THOUGHTS OF RAMESESE

The huffing and puffing of the
farmworkers
The scraping, crashing, banging
of my tomb makers.
The praying, chanting of the priests
over my body.
The whispers and groans of my
faithful servants
The crashing, shouting, banging
of people taking my gold
The excited voices of strange people
in my tomb
Then I went on a strange boat tied
to a beautiful table
And now I'm in this strange room
in the British Museum.
With strange voices and faces

Philip Purvis (10) St Peter's CE Primary School, South Weald

WOLF

Mine is the howl the snarling of the teeth
And dripping saliva dribbling from my teeth.
My teeth are as sharp as a knife.
With gums as black as ebony.
Mine is the nose that breathes in fear.
When danger comes I'm always near.
I am a wolf with eyes as brown as dust
That lurks in the wood at dusk.

Ellie Toosi (10) St Philomena's Prep School, Frinton-on-Sea

OH GRANNY

Flinging myself onto my bed
With tears streaming down my face,
Choking and gasping and thinking about it
A death in the human race.

I hated everything at that moment
Every smile was a selfish smirk,
The world was a land of shadows
Where danger and sadness lurk.

No-one could comfort or help me
An awful feeling was there,
But memories were always with me
Her laugh, her smile everywhere.

I'll never forget that dreadful moment
My mum's smile changed to tears instead,
As she put down the phone and hugged me saying
'Darling, your granny's dead.'

Even now she's still with me
Always at the back of my mind,
She helped me out with problems
And was generous, loving and kind.

Oh Granny, why did you leave me?
I really want to know why,
I'll never see you, ever again
Oh why did you have to die?

Naomi Burgoyne (10) St Philomena's Prep School, Frinton-on-Sea

ODE TO WINTER

The wind is blowing,
It may be snowing.
Trees are bare and black
Against a sky so dark.
A pond of frozen ice
I think it's very nice.

My hands are raw.
They are quite sore
Because I play outside.
Not sitting by the fireside.
The days are short and dark,
I can't spend long in the park.

Let's hurry home for tea
There's hot buns for you and me.
Spring will soon be here
With visits to the pier.

Alexander McNulty (9) St Philomena's Prep School, Frinton-on-Sea

AUTUMN

Coming along in a rush,
Shiny, woody and varnished,
Spilling from its pod and bare,
A conker lay there.

I bent down and picked it up,
And what a beautiful cup.
Shining like a golden chalice,
Straight from a palace.

At last I understand,
Hot days are over . . . and,
It's time for autumn to start,
It's autumn at last!

Thomas Davies (9) St Philomena's Prep School, Frinton-on-Sea

ODE TO WINTER

Dew glistens on the cobwebs
Icicles hang down from the eaves,
The chilly winds and cold frost,
Put an end to autumn leaves.

The warm fires brighten the drizzle
They crackle hiss and sizzle,
The colourful flames rise high,
To the wet and cold night sky.

Every day the bitter winds
Blow and gust through the door
I think about every night,
The very cold wet and poor.

The bitter morning sunshine
The cold damp air,
Think about the chilled animals
Horses, sheep, fox and hare.

Rabbits run into their burrows
Moles climb to their ground,
Hedgehogs hibernate till winter's over
Fast asleep not making a sound

Clare Mainstone (10) St Philomena's Prep School, Frinton-on-Sea

A WINTER SONNET

Winter nights are longer
Days get shorter.
Wind is howling in and out
Bare branches all about.
Dew on grass, cobwebs glitter
Winter storms are very bitter.
Temperature lowers, snow on the ground,
Slippery silver white carpets abound.
Icicle glimmering and clinging to eaves
In and out houses pathways weave.
Animals snug in hibernation
Green shoots wait in hesitation.
Snow and ice slowly melt away
Warm spring sunshine is on its way.

Fiona Bates (10) St Philomena's Prep School, Frinton-on-Sea

ODE TO WINTER

The snow is falling upon the grass
We all wonder how long it will last
The birds are looking for things to eat
The snow is crisp beneath my feet
I start to run and head for home
To sit by my fire all alone.

Bare branches blowing up and down
Snow will cover them when the time is near
Birds are pecking scraps everywhere
Berries on the holly appearing everywhere
Chirping birds sing in the branches
Sometimes blackbirds, sometimes robins
Pecking in and out the snow
It will be time to go on home

Sophie Williams (9) St Philomena's Prep School, Frinton-on-Sea

BIRTHDAYS

I like birthdays
I have one every year
And each time that it comes near
I jump up and cheer.

I like birthdays
The postman calls at dawn
With lots of cards and presents
Each year since I was born.

I like birthdays
A cake with candles bright
Balloons and party poppers
To give my Nan a fright.

I like birthdays
They celebrate my birth
And every year is one more year
That I have been on Earth.

Matthew Tandy (11) St Philomena's Prep School, Frinton-on-Sea

MY BABY BROTHER

So small and so weak
So helpless he seems.
Four weeks old, he grows and grows
The smiles and cries that we know.

The little baby from above
That God gave us, to love and hug.
To see him grow into a boy.
With lots of love and joy.

James Skilling (10) St Philomena's Prep School, Frinton-on-Sea

EXCUSES!

I'm sorry I'm late for school,
Please don't say I'm a fool,
My mum killed me!
I'm sorry I'm late for school,
My dad lost his key!
I'm sorry I'm late for school,
A knight crushed our house!
I'm sorry I'm late for school,
My sister saw a mouse!
I'm sorry I'm late for school,
We saw an Indian in our swimming pool!
I'm sorry I'm late for school,
I turned into a ghoul!
I'm sorry I'm late for school,
I saw a ghost!
I'm sorry I'm late for school,
I burnt my buttered toast!
I'm sorry I'm late for school,
An alien from outer space broke into our place!
I'm sorry I'm late for school,
A church fell on my face!
I'm sorry I'm late for school,
A wizard turned me into a toad!
I'm sorry I'm late for school,
A cowboy blocked our road!
I'm sorry I'm . . .
Yes, yes child, but can't you see?
It's very nearly half past three!

Alaric Green (8) St Thomas More RC GM Primary School,
Saffron Walden

DYING SLAVES

I see slaves being tortured to death.
I hear slaves crying for mercy.
and pleading for freedom.
The sting of a whip haunts a slave for ever.
Like rats rotting in a sewer.
A black cat wondering down an alley.
I feel furious,
I can't help in any way.

Terry Munns (11) Scargill Junior School

THE TORMENT OF SLAVERY

The window in my mind
Opens to the world of slavery
The roots of Slavery
Are based on gold
I see shadows of pain in their eyes
In the heart of the fires of hell
The memories of Slavery live on:
Will it stop?
They are trapped
Like animals in a cage
Gnawing to get out
Their bodies are welded to slavery
But their souls will always be free
The word 'Slavery'
Sends a shiver down my spine
The agony they endured
Like being dissected alive
Only death brings freedom.

Jemma Addinall (11) Scargill Junior School

THE CURSE ON SLAVES

I see slaves working on plantations
Wounds looking like a mangled hedgehog
Like a dragonfly
With its legs being pulled off one by one
There is a sound of slaves, begging for support
Shameful thoughts of my people flood though
My head.

Carl Orriss (11) Scargill Junior School

THE BLUES

I sit by the calm, quiet river
Up in the sky the clouds are floating along.
The juice oozes from a blueberry
Like paint dripping from a bottle.
I see a blue bird to bring me happiness.

Amy Cook (11) Scargill Junior School

A WORLD OF HATE

Slaves suffer like tormented rats.
White people treat slaves like scum.
Is it real, or is it just a nightmare?
My mind see racism and cruelty.
Why is the world full of hatred?

Christopher Bottoms (11) Scargill Junior School

THE UNIMAGINABLE FEELING OF BEING A SLAVE

As I look back I see captors
Like tigers pouncing on the children
As their families watch in despair.
The slaves are in an endless
frightening tunnel.
A slave is like a leper
Who never regains it's feelings.
The horrific sound of slaves
Crying for their family.
It is shameful to admit that
England dealt in slavery.

Amy Cook (11) Scargill Junior School

THE HORROR OF BEING A SLAVE

They limped for miles non stop.
In ships chained together.
Sold like toys in a shop.
In the plantation toil so laborious.
Like a water-mill never stopping.
In the end they're like worn out tin soldiers.
Is this the way God intended the English to treat
their fellow men.

David Barber (11) Scargill Junior School

SLAVES IN PAIN

Beyond their peaceful homes,
Slaves are caught.
They are whipped and stripped,
They must feel like striking out.
While a slave gets shipped away,
A tear runs down the mother's cheek.
They're treated like mud on my shoes.
Like a gun shot wound through the heart.
Slaves are dying.
I wish I could reach out and help.

Mark Townley (10) Scargill Junior School

THE DEMONS OF EVIL

In the land where evil dwells
Slaves are whipped
As they're treated like fat on bacon
They're trapped in a black hole
But there's no exit
I feel angry and appalled.
Adults work hard as children cry for freedom
Like a cannon about to explode
Slaves are swept to different cultures.
Their bodies may be sold to slavery
But their spirits are free.

Laura McLeod (11) Scargill Junior School

SLAVERY

In my mind's eye I see slaves,
They suffer at the hands of the owner.
They've lost their freedom,
Like a blind mouse trapped in a mousetrap.
Will they ever see the light of day again?

Christopher Ager (11) Scargill Junior School

THE TEA BAG

Someone's hand comes in and takes me out
I'm fresh from the box square or round
Into a mug or cup I go
Boiling water from the kettle covers me
You can have me with a slice of lemon, semi skimmed, or virtually fat
                                                                                  free milk
A prod here a prod there then I'm lifted out high in the air
My shape has changed I'm not square or round
I'm all squished up and dripping brown.
              drip drop drip.

Rebecca Aldham (11) Towers Junior School

CATS

Wouldn't you like to be a cat
To sleep all day in a hat
Rolling over in the sun
Maybe they'll go for a little run
Stop now and then to have a wash
They always like to look very posh
They'll sit on your lap be stroked and purr
But when they get up all that's left is fur
Wouldn't you love to lay
      All day
Sometimes go out to jump and play
Big green eyes to see in the dark
This is the best time for having a lark
They seem to sleep with one ear pricked
Don't stop eating till the dish is licked
This is the sort of life to lead
All the luxury you'd ever need.

Nicola Fry (9) Westerings Primary School

ANCIENT EGYPT

There is a place far away where it is hot
and sunny every day, there is a river
called the Nile that flooded for
quite a while.
Poor people buried in sand,
while Kings and Princes in pyramids
grand.
Secret tombs,
hidden treasures.
Jewellery, gems and other pleasures.
On papyrus sheets the scribes would
write.
The workers worked from dawn till night.

Emma Stone (9) Westerings Primary School

WAR

War one,
War two, Did the war affect you?

Is it money,
Is it gold,
Your heart must be very cold.

Leather hand,
Metal bones
War brings death and broken homes.

In German hay,
I sat here and lay,
Wishing the day away.

Thinking if my family,
Was dead or alive,
It could be a bad surprise.

Army, army everywhere,
Did the Germans really care?

Jonathan Harbage (11) Westerings Primary School

BY THE POND

Little black tadpoles,
Eating the weed,
Grow into frogs,
Before they breed.

Water is cool,
Down by the pool,
Swimming around,
Making no sound, little black tadpoles.

Frog spawn jelly,
Floating in the pond,
Pond skaters skating,
All over the place.

Frogs croaking,
Lilies soaking
In the sun,
Warming up everyone.

Nicola Hollingdale (9) Westerings Primary School

MY NEW FRIEND

Jack frost came to my garden,
I saw him in a tree;
He looked so very lonely
I asked him in to tea

He thanked me very kindly
And said that would be nice
He did not sit upon a chair
But on a block of ice

He liked the cake and ice-cream,
They were his favourite food.
I said that he could stay the night
He said I wish I could.

But Jack had lot's of work to do,
He hoped to call again:
He came last night and wrote thank-you
Across my window pane.

Fiona MacDonald (9) Westerings Primary School

UNDER THE BED

Under the bed there are ghosts.
Under there, Don't get too close,
'Cos they'll give you a scare,
       Please beware!
They'll give you a scare.
Your eyes will pop out.
You'll want to get out.
You'll want to shout,
But it just won't come out.
You jump out of bed,
Clearing your head,
Thinking it's just a dream.
Then one jumps out and gives you a fright,
Like the ghost of the night.
Then you run away quickly with
All of your might.

Louise Longhurst (11) Wentworth Primary School

SEASONAL JOYS

Summer, winter,
Autumn, spring
Whatever the season
I want to sing!
Because morning or evening
Day or night
There are always fresh beauties
To bring delight

Helen Hill (8) Wentworth Primary School

MY DOG

Golly gosh there's my dog
We found him in the fog
He's black and white
But that's alright
We called him Tosh
It's not too posh
He's a Border Collie
And such a wally
Should have herded sheep
But they ended up in a heap
I love my dog lots and lots
Even though he drives me dots.

Kirsty Ferris (11) Wentworth Primary School

THIS IS MY POEM

This is my poem, I made it myself
to show I am well and in good health.
It's not about demons or robbers in caves,
it's not about Kings, Queens, servants or slaves.

This is my poem, I made it myself,
it's either a fairy, pixie or an elf.
I chose a fairy, a pretty one of course
and I'll make her some dinner with my apple sauce.

This is my poem, I made it myself,
and I'll put it on the top bit of my shelf.
The fairy I told you died pretty quick,
because she hated my sauce and was quite sick.

This is my poem, I made it myself,
but it may not give me a lot of wealth.
The funeral of the fairy was at eleven
and the funeral lasted until seven.

Georgina Privett (10) Westminster Prep School

THERE ARE NOISES EVERYWHERE

There are noises everywhere
From the crashes of thunder
To the swish of hair
From the rustle of leaves
To the peals of laughter at the fair
The noise of a pen writing on paper
Scritch, scratch, scritch, scratch
And the rusty old gate swinging in the air
Click, clack, click, clack
The ticking of a clock
Tick, tock, tick, tock
And the buskers playing in the square
De da dum de da, De da dum de do
From the scraping of a chair
To the pop music blaring
From the engine roaring
To the sound of silence
There are noises everywhere.

Louisa McKenzie (11) Woodford County High School

SPIDER

Spider spins a silky web
In a corner of a tree.
He waits for a juicy fly
And eats it for his tea.

Spider eats a butterfly
Spider eats a fly
Spider eats what ever he can
Whatever is passing by

Bee Bee flying around
Fly, fly up in the sky
Spider waiting in his web
To catch a juicy fly.

Rebecca Garland (8) Writtle Junior School

SPIDERS SCAMPERING

Spiders, scampering
on spindly legs,
Spiders, making egg sacks
in which to lay their eggs.

Spiders, crawling
everywhere,
Spiders, legs
splayed out here and there.

Spiders, making webs
to catch their food,
Spiders, putting cleaners
in a bad mood.

Spiders, catching
their food which are flies,
Spiders, seeing everything
with eight eyes.

Thomas Gibb (9) Writtle Junior School

BUTTERFLIES

Butterfly flying in the sky
Butterfly flying upon high
Flapping and flying all day long
She glides and flies and sings a song

Where she'll fly next nobody knows
She never stops she only goes
Taking nectar from the flowers
Whiling away lonesome hours

Her feelers feel and smell galore
She sucks nectar and looks for more
Tortoiseshell, small white, ringlet too
And don't forget the common blue

They come out of a chrysalis
Caterpillar life they don't miss
With furry tummies and small legs
The mum can die once she's laid her eggs

Katrina Soderquest (9) Writtle Junior School

BUTTERFLY POEM

Caterpillar's change through metamorphosis
From tiny eggs to Butterflies called
Tortoises

Soon the caterpillar will be in its cocoon
Sleeping through night, day and noon

The cocoon is made from silken threads
To make the caterpillar have a comfy bed

When the Butterfly hatches out in glee
It is coloured really beautifully

Butterflies are symmetrical on both sides
And have beautiful colours to make them
Recognised

Annalise Long (10) Writtle Junior School

INFORMATION

We hope you have enjoyed reading this book - and that you will continue to enjoy it in the coming years.

If you like reading and writing poetry drop us a line, or give us a call, and we'll send you a free information pack.

Write to

        Poetry Now (Young Writers) Information
        1-2 Wainman Road
        Woodston
        Peterborough
        PE2 7BU